the Art *of*
Authenticity

the Art of Authenticity

TOOLS TO BECOME AN
AUTHENTIC LEADER
AND YOUR BEST SELF

Dr. Karissa Thacker

WILEY

Cover design: Paul McCarthy
Cover image: Real sheep: © Getty Images / Fuse
           Plastic sheep: © Getty Images / Juzant

Published by John Wiley & Sons, Inc., Hoboken, New Jersey.

Published simultaneously in Canada.

For general information about our other products and services, please contact our Customer Care Department within the United States at (800) 762-2974, outside the United States at (317) 572-3993 or fax (317) 572-4002.

Wiley publishes in a variety of print and electronic formats and by print-on-demand. Some material included with standard print versions of this book may not be included in e-books or in print-on-demand. If this book refers to media such as a CD or DVD that is not included in the version you purchased, you may download this material at http://booksupport.wiley.com. For more information about Wiley products, visit www.wiley.com.

Library of Congress Cataloging-in-Publication Data:

Names: Thacker, Karissa, author.
Title: The art of authenticity: tools to become an authentic leader and your
   best self/Dr. Karissa Thacker.
Description: Hoboken: Wiley, 2016. | Includes index.
Identifiers: LCCN 2015040938| ISBN 9781119153429 (hardback) | ISBN
   9781119153467 (ePDF) | ISBN 9781119153542 (ePub)
Subjects: LCSH: Leadership—Psychological aspects. | BISAC: BUSINESS &
   ECONOMICS/Leadership.
Classification: LCC HD57.7 .T4643 2016 | DDC 658.4/092—dc23 LC record available at
   http://lccn.loc.gov/2015040938

Printed in the United States of America

10 9 8 7 6 5 4 3 2 1

*This book is dedicated to my clients, who struggle
to create extraordinary business results* and *be true
to themselves. It is not an easy struggle,
but it is well worth it.*

CONTENTS

CONTENTS

PREFACE

If you would have told me three years ago that I would be writing a book on authenticity, of all things, I would have laughed. The topic made me feel vaguely uncomfortable. I have often felt that being my true self was in conflict with meeting my goals, which were also a part of me; not in big ways, but in small ways that felt slowly corrosive. (And I have never done anything remotely criminal aside from speeding.)

What changed? My intellectual and emotional curiosity about the topic got aroused during a continuing education program. After that workshop, I began to dig deeply into the work of Bill George, Robert Terry, and the foundational modern research on authenticity of social psychologists Michael Kernis and Brian Goldman. I discovered a rich body of literature and a topic that provoked incredible conversations. I started talking to my clients about the topic and trying to understand their views in casual conversations. I discovered I was not alone in this struggle to be true to myself and meet my goals, nor in feeling a vague sense of discomfort around the topic for similar reasons.

I also began to envision a view of authenticity from a psychological perspective, one that was pragmatic and designed to illuminate those "small" ways in which we choose to be true to ourselves—or not—and perhaps create room for new possibilities in those moments. Practically speaking, it also made sense that the more one contemplated authenticity in the small moments, the greater the likelihood one would be "in shape" to behave authentically in the big, defining moments. The more I read and talked with clients and colleagues, the more intrigued I was. I became haunted by the following question: How could we become more authentic through those small daily struggles in real, pressure-filled situations? Or practically speaking, how could we up our percentage of authentic actions? That question is the foundation of this book.

The point of view in this work is that authenticity is all about human possibility, creativity, expression, and freedom. Becoming more authentic is a grand concept and is far more than avoiding doing bad things like lying and cheating. The possibility is found in the midst of an honest appraisal of the real struggles and making choices that are more mindful and conscious. This book is about discovering the possibilities for you to be both authentic and successful at the same time. The book brings you the most relevant tools and insights from psychology. However, becoming a version of you that is both authentic and effective is your art to bring to the world. Hence, the title *The Art of Authenticity*.

The text is organized in three separate sections. Part 1 consists of three chapters and is titled "A New Vision of Authenticity." The goal of this section is to refine and contemporize the concept for the digital age. In Chapter 1, "The Digital Era of Freedom and Fear," the connection between authenticity and modern workplace realities is explored. Strong forces such as the flattening of hierarchy and globalization have created a macro environment in which becoming more authentic could very well be more adaptive than just doing your job and blending in. Beginning in Chapter 1 and in each subsequent chapter, the chapter closes with practical workouts designed to help leaders develop skills in becoming more authentic in real-life work situations. In Chapter 2, "Signature Contributions vs. Conformity," readers are challenged to contemplate what is unique about themselves as individuals. What is the unique combination of skills and perspective that only you can bring? It takes extra effort to tune into yourself and figure out what you really want and need to contribute. This new, practical view of authenticity requires you to go deep and think really hard about situations and who you want to be instead of just being on autopilot and conforming. Having signature contributions that are obvious when your name is mentioned is the litmus test for authenticity.

Chapter 3, "Truth, Lies, and Authenticity," brings the first foundational section of the book to a close with an exploration of overlapping and confusing terms such as truth, honesty, and transparency. We all think of transparency, truth, and honesty as being part of authentic leadership. But in reality there are lots of ways of interpreting terms such as truth, honesty, and transparency. We explore less-than-straightforward questions such as the value of being brutally honest if you know it is going to harm either a person or a business. Seeking the truth is a continual quest, and being brutally honest is a behavioral choice in a specific situation that could be harmful to others.

The second part of the book, "The Science of Authenticity," takes the reader on a journey through what we have learned about authenticity from the science of psychology. The big insight from social psychology is that authenticity is not just one thing but a multiple component variable. Authenticity consists of at least four variables, all of which have a chapter in this section. But we begin the section with Chapter 4, "Followers Beware . . . of Charisma," a look at how many people mistake charisma for authenticity. Charisma is a separate and distinct characteristic from authenticity. However, most of us have been taken in at some point by someone who was very charismatic but did not turn out to be genuine in the long run. The reality is that charismatic, larger-than-life leaders may or may not be authentic. This chapter outlines what team members should be on the alert for and notice in order to figure out whether or not their leader is actually genuine or just has a great show.

In Chapter 5, "Self-Awareness or Is it Selves Awareness?" we explore the first component of authenticity discovered in the quantitative psychological research. Not surprisingly, self-awareness is one of the components of authenticity. However, this chapter gets real and takes on the notion of one consistent self that is so prevalent in ordinary business conversations. The reality is that we all have multiple sides and facets, which are compounded by multiple role demands. Common knowledge states that people behave in certain ways due to their personalities. In reality, much of our behavior is determined by the situation. This chapter will help the reader become more authentic by developing greater selves awareness.

We delve into the second component of authenticity in "Chapter 6: Balanced Processing and Collaborative Decision Making." Balanced processing is about blending your thought process with the thought processes of others without a bias toward your view. Nothing may be more important in today's collaborative business environment than this skill of balanced processing. Balanced processing is a part of good decision making as well as authenticity. The construct is fully explored through the use of real-world examples. Readers are challenged to develop their own balanced processing skills through seeking out opposing views and actually listening carefully.

The third component of a psychological model of authenticity is relational transparency. The realities of transparency in the real world are explored in Chapter 7, which is titled "Relational Transparency and Honest Conversations." Why can it be so difficult to have an honest conversation in a modern corporation about what is really happening with your project or the business as a whole? The case study of Alan Mulally and the remarkable turnaround at Ford is used as an example of the power of honest conversations. The chapter also explores how the rules are changing regarding the emotional transparency that is expected of leaders about who they are as people, which may not be directly relevant to business issues. The times are changing quickly and the rules and expectations regarding both intellectual and emotional transparency are in a state of flux.

The fourth component of a psychological model of authenticity is explained in Chapter 8, "Internalized Moral Perspective/An Active Unique GPS System." This chapter explains the terrain of moral psychology and helps the reader make sense of both moral and immoral behavior. It is only through a willingness to look at our own self-righteous thinking and feelings that we can actually live in accordance with our own values. The chapter draws heavily on the work of Jonathan Haidt, who has clarified that morality is primarily driven by intuition and gut reactions, not cognition.

In the third and final part of the book, "The Master Class," we delve into the more complex insights that must be translated into daily behavior in order to become a more authentic leader as you are facing the pressures of day-to-day situations. Chapter 9 kicks off the final section and is titled "The Centrality of Conscious Choice." We all make thousands of choices every day. Many of them are conscious, and perhaps more are totally unconscious. The path toward greater authenticity requires that leaders become more conscious of all the choices they are making. This chapter debunks the idea that you have little control over your real self. Readers are challenged through the work of Dr. Ellen Langer on scientific mindfulness to choose more and react less.

Next, we move from conscious choice into the realm of organizational culture in Chapter 10, "How to Read Culture Like an Anthropologist." Organizations are highly variable in terms of cultures, and authentic leaders must bring great skill in understanding organizations as cultures. You are both authentic and/or effective in a specific organizational culture. Finding a good cultural fit is critical if you are to grow as an authentic leader. Authentic leaders have the ability to shape the culture, but not if they don't understand it as it is. The reader will leave Chapter 10 with a new appreciation for making sense of human behavior in organizations through the lens of organizational culture.

We move from organizational culture to the topic of paradox in Chapter 11, "How to Make Peace with Paradox." Real people and real decisions require us to make sense of paradox or seemingly contradictory notions. Both people and situations are inherently paradoxical. The chapter draws heavily on the work of Robert Quinn, who has identified leadership as a state of mind that is other focused instead of self-focused. All of us can shift from self-focus to other focus with skill if we know how to make peace with the paradox that is us. Human beings are by nature capable of great, unselfish feats and myopic, self-oriented behavior within the same hour. This chapter will provide readers with tools to manage their own peculiar paradoxical human nature.

For the final chapter of the book, Chapter 12, "How to Ferociously Seek the Truth When Everyone Is Framing and Spinning," I saved the best and most complicated for last. We delve into the workplace realities and power dynamics that give rise to all the framing and spinning. The key to seeking and getting the truth is to understand that it is the leader's responsibility to create a climate in which people are safe to tell the truth. Every gesture counts, as people are always calculating just how much they can trust their leaders. Practicing virtues like truth-telling and creating trusting environments is extremely rewarding. However, we may be moving too fast to notice at times. In the final section, readers are challenged to notice what happens on an internal level when they witness virtuous behaviors like truth-telling.

In aggregate, it is my goal that you as the reader are both challenged and supported in the quest toward becoming more authentic as a leader.

PART I

A New Vision of Authenticity

1

THE DIGITAL
ERA OF FREEDOM
AND FEAR

In effect, managing one's self demands that each knowledge worker think and behave like a chief executive officer. Furthermore, the shift from manual workers who do as they are told to knowledge workers who have to manage themselves profoundly challenges the social structure. Every existing society, even the most individualistic one, takes two things for granted, if only subconsciously; that organizations outlive workers and most people stay put. But today, the opposite is true. Knowledge workers outlive organizations and they are mobile. The need to manage oneself is therefore creating a revolution in human affairs.[1]

—Peter Drucker

Excelling at leading a business is an amazing gift. We have lost sight of the enormous contribution made by the vast majority of people who lead organizations that produce goods or services. I have always been amazed by the extraordinary talents of my clients.

Laughingly, I call them all action addicts. Truly authentic leaders are people who know how to make sure the stuff that really matters gets done <u>and</u> raise the performance of thousands of people (including themselves) to a higher standard <u>through their presence, impact, and well-chosen actions.</u>

I've learned from some of the best. What have I learned? Finding the balance between being yourself and relating effectively within a demanding context is not easy. Successful organizations are social systems with tremendous pressures toward specific behaviors that have led to the organization's success in the past.[2] "Just be who you are and live your values" sounds deceptively simple. Leaders must pay attention, adjust, and adapt to complex situations both inside the organization and in the marketplace or they will not be leaders for long. Finding the balance between being your true self and adapting to the cacophony of pressures is a complex, very personal equation. Platitudes are just not enough.

We live in a time of intense pressure to produce quarterly earnings amid constant, unpredictable market forces. For every glitzy empty suit that you've seen on television being carted away for fraud or exiled for a golden office toilet, I have had the privilege of working closely with at least 20 other talented executives. The less glitzy ones that you do not see on television are struggling to embody their values, lead toward the common good, and deliver economic results in an incredibly turbulent global marketplace. This book is an invitation to join the struggle and become one of "them" in a good way.

☙

THE CALL TO AUTHENTICITY

We are all leaders and we are all followers in this digital era. Things have changed a lot during the first 15 years in this new century. In 1999, Peter Drucker, the sage of the business world, predicted that we would all need to learn to manage ourselves like Da Vinci, Mozart, and Napoleon.

The truth is that we all need to learn to lead ourselves and answer the call to be authentic. The essence of authenticity is being yourself fully.

It requires courage. Being an authentic leader is not just about making the right ethical decision when the heat is on. It is primarily about doing the work every day to bring your best self forward into the world so that you are in shape when the heat is on and the pressure is high. Being authentic is just like being in shape physically. It is a daily decision and there is no substitute for doing the work. This book serves as a guidebook for those who want to do the work.

Why does authenticity matter now? How is authentic leadership different from leadership—or the lack thereof we hear so much about? We live in an era in which fear is a huge force, and we hear about it all the time due to our unprecedented ability to communicate incessantly. The situational press of fear, negativity, and cynicism is deafening. The World Economic Forum lists deepening income disparities, persistent structural unemployment, diminishing confidence in economic policies, and a lack of leadership as part of its top 10 global trends for the year 2015.

We're not living in easy times, but when have they ever been easy? The challenges are just different. One hundred years ago in 1915, the Great War was raging. Unlike in 1915, blending in below the radar with a predictable job may not be possible today.

⟨∽⟩

On Becoming More Authentic

Becoming more authentic may be a key to reaching your external dreams and achieving internal well-being. People who have something unique to say and are willing to step up and say it are increasingly finding success. Many would not have predicted the election of Barack Obama in 2008. Obama used his personal story and the facts of his biography in an inspired, authentic manner. The electorate responded. Obama's message of personal authenticity resonated deeply with the younger demographic. Regardless of your opinion regarding Obama's results as president, his story is indicative of someone who led himself and chose his own path. Choosing your own path with an understanding of external forces is at the heart of psychological authenticity. The vast majority of people may never choose to lead themselves and be authentic. But a percentage of people in every generation do choose the path.

Authenticity is not a new idea. Historically, being authentic generally meant being true to yourself. Being genuine or real. It has generally been accepted across philosophical traditions and cultures to be a state to which one aspires. It is assumed that being authentic is a good thing. It's likely that when you describe someone as "authentic," you admire them.

The drive toward being genuine or real also appears to be innate. We first experience the awareness that we are being real or being fake in early adolescence. Research by developmental psychologist Susan Harter clarifies that adolescents report negative psychological states associated with being fake and prefer to be themselves.[3]

So why does authenticity really matter now? Perhaps it is adaptive in the external environment to be authentic for the first time. To be sure, the forces toward conformity that are part of the human condition still exist. However, the opportunities for jobs in which you just do the same thing every day are going away. The Industrial Era was a time of great opportunity and a level of financial security if you were willing to consistently work hard at basically the same thing every day. Our current world places little value on rote tasks that can be easily accomplished through the use of technology. You are more likely to be successful in the world of work and leadership by being authentic as it is defined in this book than by blending in and going along with the crowd.

The drive toward authenticity requires you—like Mozart, Da Vinci, and Napoleon—to think for yourself. It requires you to do the hard work of figuring out what you really, really want to do. You must dig in and notice your passions, your strengths, your shortcomings, and relentlessly pursue opportunities.

Success will go to the people who know how to work with other people in order to get difficult and important things done. The level of psychological sophistication and depth required to connect, relate, and achieve in partnership with others has escalated in the last 15 years. Due to flatter organizations, we no longer have role authority to rely on— role authority meaning the assumption that people will just do what we say. Having or nurturing new ideas, collaborating to win, and figuring out how to do what no one else has figured out how to do yet are the winning strategies in this new world. Cultivating authenticity and tuning into yourself in your world at a deeper level are required to accomplish such lofty goals on a daily basis.

People across the world can access your social media posts—and you can access theirs. The notion of privacy seems more of a fantasy than a reality. Anyone anywhere can capture your worst moments of any day on a video or a photo. But you can also use those same tools to craft relationships and learn in ways that were unthinkable just a few years ago.

Cultivating authenticity is the key to flourishing in our current era of freedom and fear. The authentic are brave enough to be themselves despite all of the fear within as well as all of the fear in the atmosphere.

To be sure, being authentic sounds really trite as an answer to the compelling workplace dilemmas of today. Just be yourself. Know yourself. Haven't we all heard this before in one form or another? But what if truly being yourself is much easier to say than to actually do? What if truly being yourself requires particular focused work, unusual idiosyncratic discipline, and keen powers of self-observation? What if authenticity is the key to flourishing in this digital era of freedom and fear?

The idea of authenticity can be traced back to ancient Greek philosophy with often-repeated phrases such as *know thyself*. However, there is no coherent, consistent or well-organized body of knowledge on authenticity. The knowledge base on authenticity is more like unconnected islands that address the concept in a fragmented fashion.

This text will connect the islands of knowledge on authenticity in the psychological literature and the practice-oriented leadership literature from the world of business. Advances in the last 15 years in the world of scientific psychology have made it clear that being authentic and being an authentic leader are not just one thing. Authentic leadership in psychological terms consists of multiple, interrelated, complex skills and ways of making sense of the world. From the pragmatic, business-practice–oriented leadership literature, authors Bill George, Gareth Jones, and Rob Goffee have challenged leaders to ask themselves tough questions. George focused on values by challenging leaders to find their *True North*.[4] Jones and Goffee have asked thousands of leaders *Why Should Anyone Be Led By You?*[5]

In the modern workplace and in casual conversations, we are much more comfortable discussing the person who's perceived as a fake. Listen carefully to conversations and you will notice the notion of authenticity mostly discussed in the context of who *lacks it.*

What you probably haven't heard is someone pondering their *own* authenticity—or lack thereof. When was the last time you heard someone admit they behaved like a fake to get something they wanted? Have you ever heard an adult say "I'm struggling to be more authentic"? It doesn't happen often.

What exactly does it mean to be authentic in psychological terms? What have we learned in the last 15 years? Far from letting it all hang out and just being yourself, the notion of being authentic that is becoming clearer consists of at least four interrelated variables: "selves" awareness, unbiased processing, appropriate transparency, and concordance between behavior and values. Each of these ideas is fully explained in this book, and exercises are presented to help you develop each of the big four skills that comprise authenticity in psychological terms.

Each of the big four skills requires a depth of understanding about the environment, or as we psychologists like to say, the context. Warren Bennis defined leaders as people who master the context as opposed to being mastered by their context. Understanding and feeling the pressure of a situation is a fact of life, but allowing the situation to determine who you are and how you will respond is a choice. Strong situational pressures are always present, and leaders find ways to use the strong forces of their particular time and situation. What is it that is unique about this moment in history?

⟨⟩

The Particular Challenges of Now and How Did We Get Here?

History's great achievers—a Napoleon, a Da Vinci, a Mozart—have always managed themselves. That, in large measure, is what makes them great achievers. Now, most of us, even those of us with modest endowments, will have to learn to manage ourselves.

—*Peter Drucker, HBR, 1999*[6]

It was October of 1999. I was 34 four years old. I was a management consultant at a global psychologically based consulting firm. I had just settled into seat 10E on my flight to Minneapolis when I read the words above from Drucker's now classic article titled "Managing Oneself." I was flying to Minneapolis to work with my largest client, Best Buy Corp.

It was the era of the big-box retailer. Consumer electronics was hot. New gadgets were flying off the shelf, and Best Buy's stock was flying high. The very air smelled like opportunity, and dot-coms were promising prosperity without end. What did Drucker mean when he said that people of average ability would have to manage themselves like Mozart or Napoleon? It appeared to me that plenty of people with modest endowments or average abilities were making plenty of money following pretty obvious paths. Since I'd been recently promoted to senior consultant in my firm, I considered myself to be among them.

I literally highlighted several paragraphs of Drucker's eloquent prose (there was no iPad then), thinking how useful the ideas would be in the leadership development work that I was doing at Best Buy. I would sound very cutting edge and smart quoting Peter Drucker. All of my clients would have heard the name and have a vague sense that he was important.

I read deeper. Drucker was saying that we all should be able to answer the following five questions in really practical terms:

- What are my strengths?
- How do I work best?
- What are my values?
- Where do I belong?
- What can I contribute?[8]

Drucker envisioned a world in which average knowledge workers knew their strengths and weaknesses, in which kinds of situations they could contribute the most, and deeply understood both their own values and the values of the organization in which they worked. With this insight, workers could then determine how to contribute the most.

It was essentially up to the workers to figure all this out, as managers of the future would no longer be spelling all this out with their job descriptions and management by objectives. The critical-thinking psychologist within me thought, *There is no way that the vast majority of people will be able to chart their own course and manage themselves.* Everything we know about human behavior clearly points out the power of conformity, role, and structure. The vast majority of people simply want to blend in, find a good job, and follow a predictable, stable path. A rather dark view but nonetheless data driven.

The view in 1999 was bright, and looking back we had no clue what was coming with the advent of the new millennium. The Industrial Revolution had created opportunities particularly in the manufacturing sector in the last half of the twentieth century. During that time period an average person could earn financial security by conforming and doing as one was told. One could get a job in manufacturing at General Motors or Ford, afford to send the kids to college, and receive a great pension. It appeared that each generation was going to be more upwardly mobile than the last. The post–World War II boom brought many happy days, and the United States rose to both unparalleled economic prosperity and power on the world stage.

Fast-forward 15 years from seat 10E on that flight to Minneapolis and I have been an entrepreneur inventing and managing myself and my brand for 12 years. I personally have been on at least three different paths in the last 15 years, none of which turned into a predictable one with a cozy retirement package. The predictable, smooth path that I had imagined on that flight has not been my reality for the last 15 years.

Within the last 15 years in the broader world, we have been through the tragedy of 9/11, countless corporate ethical debacles including Enron, a real estate market collapse, the meltdown of the financial markets in 2008, a stubbornly high unemployment rate in the United States, skyrocketing youth unemployment in parts of Europe, the longest war in American history, globalization including the rise of India and China as forces to be reckoned with on the world and economic stages, and unprecedented technological developments. These changes and developments at the macro level have implications for all of us as individuals and the ways in which we need to think about developing ourselves.

The Dawn of the Digital Age

If you listen to the news, you have likely heard that we are in the midst of what the vast majority of pundits call the Digital Age. Since the year 2000, the workplace has been shaped by six major forces. There are others, but these six have affected the workplace in tangible, easily observable ways that I notice every day. The top six are:

1. The smartphone
2. Rise of social media
3. Pace of change in the markets
4. Flattening of hierarchy
5. Generational shifts
6. Layoffs and downsizing

Who knows when we truly entered the Digital Age? However, the importance of the first item—the smartphone—in changing our culture is not debatable. Do you remember where you were when you first saw the iPhone? Or where you worked when you really started to want one? For me, it was a hot April day in 2007 in the great state of Texas. It was the last day of a long week of corporate training at the Southern Methodist University Business School. AT&T was launching its signature management training program that week titled T University.

I was serving as an executive coach facilitating teams during business simulations and helping people figure out what they needed to work on as a leader. In Drucker's terms, my job was to help people figure out how to leverage their strengths, be clear about their values, and figure out how they could best contribute.

The room was quiet. The new CEO, Randall Stephenson, was about to speak to the class. Randall is tall and has a commanding presence, but he took the room by simply holding up his new iPhone and saying that the small device was the key to growth in the new AT&T near term. He painted a picture of a world in which accessing the Internet from your phone was going to be more frequent than from your computer. Believe it or not, it sounded far-fetched at the time. Now the smartphone is ubiquitous, and it has literally changed the world and the workplace.

Randall also mentioned an app I had not heard of before that day that his daughter was using. The app was called Facebook. The social media revolution was upon us. Our social media profiles are part of who we are these days. Few of us are very far from our smartphones and we can, of course, friend, link in, and tweet from our smartphone.

Along with instant communication and information, it seems that markets are in a constant state of flux. Samsung came on strong and has given Apple serious competition in the smartphone arena within the last five years. Canadian company Research in Motion, now named Black-Berry Ltd., is hanging on by a thread. Remember the BlackBerry? Most leaders have become accustomed to the fact that markets appear, change, and disappear overnight. Leaders must struggle to see around the corners for their very survival.

The pace of change is intense and the price of not seeing the next big change coming can be severe. For example, on November 10, 2008, Circuit City stores, Inc. filed for bankruptcy. Walmart and other competitors, many of them Internet-based, had been gaining market share for the previous several years. According to the press, the era of the big-box retailer was officially over. Just a few years earlier, Circuit City had been widely touted as one of the best American companies by a respected academic from Stanford named Jim Collins. His canonical work *Good to Great*[7] was published in 2001. Circuit City figured prominently in the pages of Jim Collins' book as a shining example of a company that had gone from good to great. In less than 10 years, Circuit City had gone from good to great to gone.

Middle management barely exists anymore. Large organizations are a lot flatter. In a world in which everyone has access to information, you do not need the middle management layer to pass on the instructions and wisdom from the top of the hierarchy. Zappos says it no longer needs hierarchy. Google has rotating leadership based on projects.

Decisions are increasingly made in the context of teams that form quickly for the purpose of understanding or resolving an issue, and then dissolve. Effective leaders take initiative and bring the right people together to tackle specific issues. Amy Edmondson of the Harvard Business School refers to this process as "teaming" and presents a model in which people actively "team" with others all the time vs. serving on a permanent team.[8]

I have a conversation at least once a week with at least one client in a large organization who says, "I do not know how much more I can do with how much less." Layoffs, downsizing, and reductions in force (RIFs) were a part of the news every day for a five-year period between 2008 and 2013. No one was immune. Every company large and small was forced to cut fixed costs in order to stay competitive. People are a big cost. Technology also replaced repetitive jobs at a breathtaking speed.

Finally, generational shifts are clear and present in the current workplace. Authors Ron Zemke, Claire Raines, and Bob Filipczak describe the workplace as the clash of boomers, Gen Xers, and Gen Yers.[9] Gen Xers were born between 1965 and 1980. Generation Y, more commonly referred to as the millennial generation, is often described as being born between 1981 and 2000. The baby boomers, born between 1946 and 1964, are aging and staying in the workforce longer than any previous generation. There are different opinions out there about which year started which generation. However, the reality is that it is possible to have people between the ages of 25 and 60 collaborating and teaming up to tackle a problem. You can't assume that the 60-year-old is the boss. There may not be a boss; and the older, more experienced person may not be the best person for the leadership role. It is not unusual to be reporting to someone younger than you in some capacity. The digital natives, born around the year 2001, are coming next.

It is a brave, new, complicated terrain from a human interaction perspective. It is not so easy to understand exactly where everyone fits, when the right time to retire is, or if you will ever retire.

Facebook stock traded at $81.00 per share and Mark Zuckerberg was 15 years old when I was on that plane to Minneapolis in 1999. Today, Apple Inc. is the largest, most profitable company in the world. In 1999, General Motors topped the list of the Fortune 500. In 2009, GM declared bankruptcy and needed a government bailout to survive.

༺❧༻

DIGITAL ERA = FEAR + FREEDOM

The Digital Era is here in full force, and we would all do well to stop looking for a predictable path. Those who desire to lead and be authentic must chart their own course. Drucker was right, and so was I. Drucker was right in that we all need to learn to manage ourselves like Mozart and Da Vinci. I was right in that the forces of human nature toward conformity and playing it safe are strong. Many people are struggling to find their way in this ambiguous new world. Managing ourselves is not enough. We must learn to lead ourselves and have the courage to be authentic. The idea of authenticity is in the zeitgeist as people use the word to describe everything from a voice to the experience of buying a car. Marketing researchers James Gilmore and Joseph Pine[10] tell us that authenticity is what consumers really want.

Many of us have more freedom than ever in the developed world. However, it is not so easy to have the courage to speak up and be true to yourself. It can feel as if your job could be at risk at almost any time as we have all watched highly talented, qualified people be downsized due to harsh economic conditions and unforeseen crises. This relatively new twenty-first century has turned into the Digital Era of Freedom and Fear. The fear that people feel in the workforce is so strong that sometimes it is hard to see the freedom. Everyone can remember where they were on September 11, 2001. The United States was attacked, which seemed unthinkable at the time. Afterward, we all believed another attack on American soil was imminent. The terrorist attack of 9/11 took a toll on our economy both literally and psychologically. We no longer felt invulnerable. The real estate and subprime mortgage mess followed. Lehman Brothers failed. If you were not laid off during all the downsizing of the last 15 years, someone close to you was.

I remember walking through Gramercy Park in New York and wondering if Morgan Stanley, one of the most venerable American financial institutions, was going down next. General Motors had to be bailed out from a near-death experience. All industries, from manufacturing to travel to distribution, have leveraged synergy. RIFs, or reductions in force, became a routine part of the news. Every major company in the United States cut the payroll line.

At the same time, we have experienced technological miracles that have changed our lives for the better. I can listen to music by all of the greatest artists in the world on a small device. I can connect with people all over the world via the Internet. Technology has continued to take over routine and repetitive tasks from the manufacturing floor to the trading floor. I can now check in at the airport and order a fast-food meal without ever interacting with a human being. The pace of this technological revolution is not slowing down. The freedom that this digital era offers is unprecedented, but people have to wonder—where and how can I add value?

RESPONDING TO THE CHALLENGES OF FREEDOM AND FEAR

It has been a hell of a start to the twenty-first century. Major big-picture events like 9/11, the banking crisis, and the housing crisis have damaged our collective optimism and sense of boundless freedom and opportunity. However, some people are seeing through the fear fog and seizing the day. All of us feel the fear, but the twenty-first century also offers freedom.

It is hard for the average human to see and experience that possibility and freedom. Barbara Frederickson has pointed out that when it comes to experiencing emotions, we have a negativity bias.[11] Particularly in threatening situations like being laid off, the emotion of fear sounds like a smoke alarm, whereas more positive emotions that might allow us to see the possibilities available to us with the newfound freedom to work wherever and whenever we want might be like soft background music.

The freedom and the potential for self-expression are both unprecedented and scary as hell. One no longer needs to sit in the office to work. We all have mobile devices that can connect us 24/7. We are free to be wherever we need to be. We can also take online courses from some of the world's best professors at leading universities. Launching a website that puts the word out that you are starting a business can be achieved in a single morning. You can take credit card payments from your iPhone with an app. It is easier than ever to start a business from an operational viewpoint. Resources are plentiful to get the basic functions covered.

Drucker predicted that we would all need to manage ourselves like Mozart, Napoleon, and Da Vinci. What exactly did Mozart, Napoleon, and Da Vinci do that we all need to be doing? Napoleon Bonaparte led France in its glory days and it is well known that he was 5'6" and rarely looked to the precedent of the past to decide what to do militarily. If you are trained at West Point today, you will study Napoleon, as well as other strategic precedents. Wolfgang Amadeus Mozart left a stable job with the archbishop in the late 1700s to freelance as a composer so he could do the work that he wanted to do in his own way. Leonardo da Vinci is well known as an artist. However, his imagination was boundless. He did not settle and just paint, though he was very good at it. He followed his curiosity into multiple fields and continued designing and dreaming up potential breakthroughs that were not nearly so practical in his day as his art. All three luminaries left multiple stable jobs! All three <u>followed a drive to be authentic, to be themselves, even when it cost them.</u>

⟡

THE WORKOUTS

- Six strong forces have emerged in the workplace during the last 15 years. Which one has affected you the most and why? Which one has affected you the least and why?

  1. The smartphone

  2. Rise of social media

  3. Pace of change in the markets

  4. Flattening of hierarchy

  5. Generational shifts

  6. Layoffs and downsizing

- Write a paragraph about the last great day you had at work. Not a good day but a *great* day. Then figure out what was unique about that day as opposed to an ordinary day. You are likely to find clues in your paragraph about your strengths. Remember Drucker's admonition to know your strengths.

- The Greek root of the word *authentic* is *author*. On a practical level, being authentic means that you are the author of your own life. The notion of being self-authoring, editing, and publishing is possible in this era in a literal way as well as a metaphorical way. Psychologist Laura King (2001) has found that people are likely to experience positive psychological states as a response to the exercise below.[12] I use the exercise with the vast majority of my executive coaching clients and have discovered that each individual often gets something different out of the exercise. What will you learn as a result of the four-day experiment below?

BEST POSSIBLE SELVES EXERCISE (LAURA KING, 2001):

- Schedule 20-minute blocks of time on four consecutive days. Go to a place where you are not going to be interrupted for 20 minutes.
- Get paper and a pen. It is important that you write instead of type.
- Keep writing for 20 minutes each of the four days. Do not edit your pages.
- Keep your pages each day in a file.
- The prompt that you will respond to each day is as follows:
  Think about yourself in the future. Imagine that everything has gone as well as it possibly could. Think of this as a realization of your life dreams. Now write about what you imagined.
- Keep the notes from every day. On the fifth day, look at all of your writing in aggregate. What jumps out at you? What themes do you notice?
- Discuss with a trusted friend or colleague.

2

SIGNATURE
CONTRIBUTIONS
VS. CONFORMITY

If knowing yourself and being yourself were as easy to do as people talk about, there wouldn't be nearly so many people walking around in borrowed postures, spouting secondhand ideas, trying desperately to fit in rather than stand out.

—Warren Bennis[1]

All of my coaching clients at some point or another are subjected to what I call the George Bailey questions. George Bailey is the main character in Frank Capra's *It's a Wonderful Life.*[2] The film begins with George at his lowest point, believing that he is worth more dead than alive. That's when his guardian angel Clarence appears. Clarence shows George what the town of Bedford Falls would have been like if George had never been born. Throughout the movie, George discovers what a powerful personal impact he has had on his community and on the lives of countless individuals.

Powerful personal impact really matters in the workplace today. There is a lot of distraction and noise in the workplace that can seduce us into confusing our busyness with real productivity or impact. In the twenty-first century workplace, we need to be thinking about our impact and looking for ways to have impact constantly. Tuning into yourself with an eye toward what it is that you can contribute to a given situation is a part of the art and discipline of authenticity.

The George Bailey questions are:

> What would have happened differently in your workplace today if you had not been there?
>
> What impact did you have on that conference call, meeting, and/or project today?
>
> How would your team be affected if you were absent for a month?

At first most clients pause and say they don't know. Some, especially more senior-level people, laugh and say, "Everyone might have had a better day if I had stayed home." Provocative questions, and they do make you think. One of the frustrations of the digital workplace and knowledge work in general is that you can't always see your results. The vast majority of real work projects require so many teams and people to come together that it can be hard to see and define your added value. Tangible results eventually come from the efforts of multiple teams, individuals, and a million different interactions.

Even though it is difficult, it is important to notice where you think you have impact and where you do not, on a daily basis. It is a way of keeping yourself honest and focused. Can you point out clear, positive effects that you have had on your workplace in general, your team, or on that boring conference call?

Often, my clients say: "Karissa, you know how all those conference calls are, they start running together. Person X was showboating again and Person Y was jockeying for more money. Same old, same old."

When they give me that routine, I know they are tuning out on those conference calls. The problem with tuning out is that you can't be authentic, and you certainly can't lead from a mind-set of checked out and bored. You also can't be an authentic leader just by responding to 400 e-mails a day.

Make becoming yourself a work of art. Be proactive, create, and invent. Look for opportunities to make signature contributions that only you could make. Maybe someone else could say or do the same thing, but not with your style or point of view. How do you do that?

What is the mind-set that the authentic leader brings to the conference call, the meeting, or the performance review? If you are going to work in the morning with the goal of being authentic and making signature contributions, what qualities should you cultivate? What are the habits of people who make signature contributions and have impact rather than blend in with the crowd? All of those questions will be addressed in this chapter. There are four ways of thinking and behaving that are key in making signature contributions as a leader. You must think through and figure out how to celebrate your quirks, constantly experiment with new behaviors, embrace your weaknesses, and figure out what is meaningful for you.

⌘

CELEBRATE YOUR QUIRKS

Anybody who's attended a leadership training event in the last 20 years knows that you need to be aware of your strengths and weaknesses. We talk a lot less in leadership development about the power of quirk, a peculiarity in action, behavior, or personality. Synonyms for quirk include idiosyncrasy, peculiarity, oddity, eccentricity, or the informal term hang-up. Originally, the word was used in the sixteenth century to describe "an unexpected twist." Franklin Delano Roosevelt, who led the United States during World War II and negotiated with the likes of Stalin and Churchill, could never quite find the courage to fire the cook in the White House. Everyone, including Roosevelt, complained for years. But the cook maintained employment in the White House. An interesting and somewhat revealing quirk that Roosevelt could hold his own with Stalin but avoided a confrontation with the cook!

We are intrigued when other people demonstrate an unexpected twist, and it is time to elevate the quirk in any discussion of authentic leadership. Our quirks are often what is most interesting about us, at least to other people. The truth of the matter is that we all have quirks. However, most of us hide them out of a need to fit in or to conform. The intense force of conformity is well documented in the scientific and popular literature. People who are authentic are willing to rebel against conformity and be themselves, quirks and all. Ask yourself: What is odd or unusual about you—what are people surprised to learn about you?

Carol Gallagher[3] completed a research study of women who had broken through the glass ceiling. For every woman who had broken through to the C level, there was a signature characteristic unique to them that everyone knew about. It could be anything from high-heeled shoes to a maniacal devotion to a sports team. The specific thing or quirk was not important. What was important was that it was specific to that individual. In more contemporary times, Madeleine Albright[4] has talked openly in the press about her pins that she puts on her jacket. She has regularly referred to selecting the pin to send a message to another world leader. Powerful male leaders also have quirks. The many quirks of Steve Jobs were well documented by Walter Isaacson.[5] However, everyone knows that Jobs always wore a black turtleneck. The black turtleneck was his signature.

Here is a great example of a quirk. I used to work with a nuclear engineer named Greg who wore starched shirts and was the epitome of efficiency, crispness, and shiny military polish. He had a huge IQ and seemed to hold every screw and system in the plant in his head. Nuclear power is a zero mistake environment. At my consulting firm, we had a profile of success for nuclear power leaders titled The Right Stuff. The profile spelled out the competencies necessary to lead in a zero mistake environment. Greg epitomized the model in the way he looked, thought, and interacted with others.

Along with all the right stuff for nuclear power leadership, he had a keen ability to read other people quickly. We were fast friends. About a year into our collaboration, I went to his house for dinner. It was a typical Midwestern suburban home. Then he told me about his plans for the weekend: He was going to a Harley-Davidson convention. He had a whole new leather outfit to ride in and was thrilled to be hanging out with other bikers all weekend. His wife was going, too, as she also loved to ride and was frugal enough not to need new leathers.

I saw a whole new side of Greg that night. We laughed as he told me how different the conversations were on the biking weekends, as the diversity of people who were attracted to riding motorbikes and Harleys in particular was fascinating. I started to understand how he could read people so quickly—he was truly fascinated with all kinds of people and open to all kinds of new experiences. Interestingly enough, his quirk of hanging on his Harley with all the other biker people was one of the reasons that he was such an excellent reader of people.

What are your quirks? What is odd or unusual about you and does not fit into the way people typically perceive you? How could you reveal yourself at the right times? We get into habits and, early on in life, we learn that our quirks should be hidden. Breaking out of habits and being willing to constantly experiment is the next important quality of mind and behavioral habit of authentic leaders.

Video games, corn holing, chess, badminton, making wine, making beer, watching all of the football games at the same time on Sunday night. A hard-core operations guy who loves romantic novels. Judging beauty contests, collecting antiques, an Olympic walker, piloting a plane, fear of flying, fear of the water, fear of heights, and a terrible sense of direction are all quirks that I have observed in an executive population.

A quirk is not simply a hobby. It is something about you that is a little out of the ordinary. Quirks pique people's interest and help them realize that the box or category that they put you is not the whole story. For example, it is interesting when someone who is willing to take bold risks with billions of dollars as a venture capitalist is afraid of heights or of the water.

One last example to ponder: Being a competitive gamer is more interesting if you are a 50-year-old female than if you are a 20-year-old male. It is the unexpected that really grabs people and holds their interest.

❧

THE MORE EXPERIMENTS THE BETTER

We don't teach enough about Ralph Waldo Emerson in business schools. An American essayist, lecturer, and poet, Emerson was one of the founders of the transcendentalist movement and impacted the collective American psyche in many ways. He was actually quite successful in promoting his ideas about the importance of the individual triumphing over powerful social systems such as organized religion. Although he was quite controversial in his time, he had impact in the first half of the nineteenth century. He ruffled feathers; however, his authenticity cannot be argued.

I regularly share two quotes from Emerson with my clients: "Don't be too timid or squeamish about your actions. All life is an experiment. The more experiments you make, the better." And, "A foolish consistency is the hobgoblin of little minds."[6]

You are probably wondering what exactly a hobgoblin is. That is usually the first comment from my clients. It does not sound like a good thing! Hobgoblins are imaginary fears. They are depicted in Shakespeare as annoyances that are not to be taken seriously. I find using the term hobgoblin does get the attention of most executives as it is not a buzz word or phrase like *synergy* or *be more strategic*.

The general idea behind the hobgoblin quote is that you have to vary your game. Any notion that being authentic means being predictable and the same as everyone else should be squashed. To be sure, being consistent enough that people know they can count on you for certain things is fair. If people know that they can count on you to really listen to multiple aspects of complex issues before sharing an opinion, that is a wise consistency, not a foolish one. A wise consistency is part of the art of authentic leadership.

Authentic leadership development is not a spectator sport. Developing yourself as an authentic leader is not about sitting in a meeting and reflecting twice a month with your coach. It is about making your work life a laboratory and constantly experimenting with new behaviors. The only way to make signature contributions is to mix it up. With clients who talk a lot, I often have them slow down and listen. I often push the ones who listen well to speak up more. You can mix it up in all kind of ways. I recently advised a brilliant tax attorney to reach out and start having lunch with the human resources leaders in his division. The human resource leaders were shocked, and the brilliant tax attorney learned a lot.

Keep trying new things, and some of it will work and some of it will not. You'll begin figuring out who you are and be on the way to actually knowing yourself—as opposed to just talking about knowing yourself. It is critical that you both act in new ways and notice what works. Pausing long enough to acknowledge whether something new has worked or not is essential. The good news is that a five-minute focused analysis goes a long way.

The seven steps of authentic leadership experimentation are:

1. Try a new behavior as opposed to just thinking about it.
2. Write down on a scale of 1–10 how effective it was. Did it work?
3. How did it feel to you on an internal level? Was it awkward?
4. If you were to do it again, what would you do differently?
5. What did you learn?
6. Where else might this new behavior work or not work?
7. Repeat.

Perform these steps every day, and over time, they will become second nature or instinct. Typically, I ask my clients to try one new thing a day for five days. I also ask them to take notes on each of the seven steps for each of the five new behaviors. Then I ask them to experiment with two new behaviors every day. Over time, they are learning about themselves through setting up their own leadership lab experiments. Finding out who you really are is an active process balanced by reflection.

In the current marketplace, it is not enough for experimentation to operate at only the individual level. Constant experimentation is required at both the team and organizational levels as well. We live in an era in which you will either be disrupted or be a disruptor in many sectors of the economy. The steps above can also be applied to strategic experimentation in the following way:

1. Try a new product, service, or strategy.
2. Write down how effective it was on a scale of 1–10. You must decide how much time you are going to give it before you ask this question. It could be 90 days, or it could shorter or longer.
3. Was the product, service, or strategy true to the team's vision of the business in the marketplace? That is the authenticity question. Was it within bounds? Out of bounds? Not a good fit? Is it potentially pointing out what the business could or should become in the marketplace?

4. If you were to do it again, what would you do differently?

5. What did your team learn?

6. How else might this new product, service, or strategy be deployed? Could it potentially work in adjacent spaces?

7. Repeat.

In a recent article on chiefexecutive.net, journalist Dale Buss reported that many top executives realize the need for their companies to make disruptive strategic moves that may even cannibalize their current business. The title of the article is "9 Ways to Get the Board behind Your Disruptive Strategies." Netflix CEO Reed Hastings recently said, "We need to become HBO before HBO becomes us." So you have Netflix trying to become HBO and vice versa! Techniques recommended to CEOs in Buss's article include filling your board with flexible personalities and creating a culture of experimentation.[7]

Dealing with disruption and adapting fast affects everyone, including smaller businesses and freelancers as well. *Fast Company* has titled our current era #genflux, or Generation Flux, calling modern business pure chaos and showcasing people who are dealing with all the disruption and succeeding.[8] Maintaining an attitude of boldness, flexibility, and experimentation is important for hard-core business reasons as well as in the service of becoming an authentic leader who makes visible signature contributions.

THE UPSIDE OF YOUR WEAKNESSES

In business, we psychologists use personality assessments and 360 evaluations to help leaders understand their strengths and weaknesses. Personality inventories vary in complexity and are widespread. The 360 feedback tools are either quantitative or qualitative. Quantitative instruments ask raters who are peers, subordinates, and superiors to rate executives on a scientifically validated competency model. The qualitative 360 method involves interviewing key colleagues and asking directly for their perceptions of a person's strengths and weaknesses.

In recent years, through the contributions of thought leaders such as Donald Clifton, Marcus Buckingham, and Tom Rath, there has been an increased focus on strengths in the assessment process. Donald Clifton is often called the father of the strengths movement in psychology. Through the work of Marcus Buckingham and Tom Rath, developing strengths has become an accepted approach to talent development. The general idea is that your energy is better invested working to get even better at your strengths than working a lot just to potentially get to average on a weakness. This model resonates with most people and makes them happy when they leave a meeting. Yeah, let's focus on our strengths!

The effect of the strengths movement has been positive overall, as a balancing out needed to happen—not to mention the fact that people are much happier when they are using their strengths on a daily basis. Knowing your key strengths and using them at least 50 percent of the time is important. Your strengths are a big part of who you really are. However, your strengths are not the whole story.

As in all things, we Americans tend to move toward excess. We believe in all things—except moderation, as my European friends tease. The reality is that due to the strengths movement, many people are afraid to say "weakness" and use the euphemism "developmental area." In contrast, authentic people are willing to say they have a weakness in a safe environment. Even more important, they are aware of their weaknesses. Some weaknesses truly are developmental areas, and some are going to continue to be weaknesses. Authentic leaders know the difference between a weakness that is not going to change and one that they need to focus effort on developing. The reality is that some weaknesses can move to strengths with focused effort.

Weaknesses and vulnerabilities are underrated in the current strengths-focused environment. Authentic leaders are able to use their weaknesses to empower the team. Leaders who tend to miss the details can rely on individuals on their teams who are good at that and appreciate them for their competence. Leaders who tend to love the detail can stack their teams with people who see around corners with ease and actually listen carefully to those people. Embracing your own weaknesses as a leader allows you to see the strengths of others more clearly and elevate the whole team.

Owning weaknesses and vulnerabilities in the right way is an important part of a leader's authenticity and individuality. Research by Zenger and

Folkman has clarified that extraordinary leaders—defined as the absolute best who are in the top 10 percent when compared with all other leaders—have one or two extraordinary strengths and one or two really bad flaws.[9] Yes, people who respond to the 360 are aware enough of the flaws to ding their bosses on it during the assessment. It is a myth that extraordinary leaders are good at everything.

The biggest struggle that my clients have with vulnerability is not knowing the answer. Thinking and saying *I don't know, what do you guys think?* is a courageous act of authenticity. Most people wind up in leadership roles because they are able to figure out the answers a lot. The challenges faced by leaders today are complicated. Maintaining the façade that you know the answer is actually dangerous because that façade will keep people from telling you what you need to know to make good decisions.

People respond and connect to other people who are real, flaws and all. Leadership is fundamentally about human relationships. We follow people we trust. Brené Brown's qualitative research has made it clear that vulnerability is one of the keys to interpersonal connection that is beyond the superficial, ego-defended chatter that often passes as conversation.[10] Brown's TED talk on the power of vulnerability went viral in 2010. To date, almost 20 million people have viewed that TED talk. Clearly, it struck a chord. Many of us have a gut reaction to hide the stuff about ourselves that we think will keep other people from accepting us. In order for deeper human connection to happen, leaders must allow themselves to be really seen vs. being an image of perfection. Leaders who desire to be authentic must reframe vulnerability as being powerful in a different way than they typically think of power. The power of vulnerability is not the power of having the answer. However, the power of vulnerability may be the key to leaders unleashing the talents of their teams to discover many potential answers to complex dilemmas.

The key to staying in touch with reality regarding both your strengths and weaknesses is to invite real-time feedback. You do not have to bring a psychologist like me into the mix to receive quality feedback if you have the courage to deal with your own vulnerabilities and weaknesses on a regular basis. You have to make it easy, normal, and regular for people to give you feedback.

It will not likely be comfortable for you at first. When Cheryl Sandberg first joined Facebook as COO, she set up what she termed Feedback Fridays with the baby-faced CEO Mark Zuckerberg.[11] Sandberg was older and considerably more experienced than Zuckerberg but knew that open communication between the two of them was going to be key. Every Friday, they would meet for the purpose of Mark giving her feedback regarding what was working or not working. He, in turn, asked for feedback as well.

This real-time feedback is what happens in the most productive, authentic business alliances. It is not always the most comfortable thing to do, but it works and serves as more than an ounce of prevention. I have clients who ask their direct reports for *feedback* in every one-on-one meeting. I tell my clients not to use the word feedback. Just go for it. The term *feedback* is too abstract and laden with meaning these days. The questions that I have my clients step up and ask are:

Note this

- What am I doing or not doing that is helpful to you?
- What am I doing or not doing that is making things difficult for you?
- How is being a part of this team working for you?

The key to getting real-time feedback is that you have to be willing to be vulnerable and tolerate the discomfort long enough to hear it. Tolerating the discomfort does not involve justifying or grimacing. The key is that you have to maintain eye contact nonverbally and ask questions verbally. This exercise is not for rookies! It also is highly effective with your peers. Your peers are more likely to give you the unvarnished truth.

◈

MEANING MATTERS

What is the meaning of your work? You are not going to get an e-mail outlining the significance of your work. The yearning for meaning and significance in your work will not likely go away. Many people in your organization of at least five different generations may be struggling for an answer to the basic questions of meaning or significance. The why behind the doing really matters in human motivation. In the words of

U2, many of us still haven't found what we're looking for. You are the one with the power to contribute meaning to your work.

It is a nice fantasy to believe that the meaning of your work and life will be spelled out for you via e-mail or even snail mail. Toward the end of Monty Python's *The Meaning of Life*, a restaurant hostess opens an envelope that contains the meaning of life.[12] Finally, the answer! She opens the envelope with nonchalance and reads it. The meaning of life is: "Try and be nice to people, avoid eating fat, read a good book every now and then, get some walking in, and try and live together in peace and harmony with people of all creeds and nations." The hostess closes by sardonically saying that this answer is not going to bring people out to see the movie. Pornography would be a better bet!

Not much has changed since the 1980s, except we now know that we should eat some fat. The ever-present quest for meaning at work has cropped back up again in the form of Gen Xers and millennials pressing the issue. A recent article in *The Wall Street Journal* was titled "I Don't Have a Job. I Have A Higher Calling."[13] A job is not just a job anymore, as the leadership of all kinds of companies attempts to frame the company's core task as meaningful. Many employers are essentially trying to make an announcement to everyone to clarify exactly how their work is meaningful. It reminds me of the climactic scene in *Monty Python*.

Research has made it evident that people who are clear about a higher purpose in their work are more satisfied, engaged, and willing to go the extra mile.[14] However, the process of deriving purpose from your work is an inside job. What is meaningful for one person is not meaningful to the next. As nice as it would be to have an organization spell it out for us, it is up to us as individuals to figure out what is meaningful to us. There are no shortcuts. People who are authentic are aware of what is meaningful to them. The question is not *What is the meaning of work or life in general*? The question for people who want to become more authentic is *What is meaningful to you*?

Your signature contributions will likely come from doing things that you personally find meaningful. Research in psychology has made it clear that meaning is self-determined. How do you figure that out? You must become skilled at noticing when you feel emotions that you

connect with meaning and purpose. Positive psychologists have provided a tool to help you get started on the journey to discovering what
provides purpose and meaning for you. Christopher Peterson and
Martin Seligman completed an ambitious project that served to organize human virtue and character.[15] Years of study culminated with the
development of an assessment instrument titled the VIA strengths
finder.

But these strengths are not like strengths on corporate competency
models, such as being strategic or leading a team. These are 24 character
strengths: creativity, curiosity, judgment, love of learning, perspective,
bravery, perseverance, honesty, zest, love, kindness, social intelligence,
teamwork, fairness, leadership, forgiveness, humility, prudence, self-
regulation, appreciation of beauty and excellence, gratitude, hope,
humor, and spirituality. It is through the exercise and cultivation of
these strengths of character that we can find meaning in our work lives. An
accountant who practices the virtue of honesty and holds that dear is likely
to be doing meaningful work. An employee who sees that a new product is
not going to work and speaks up is practicing bravery, and that is likely to
be meaningful to that employee. An executive with the character strength
of forgiveness who takes a risk and hires someone who has a criminal past
is likely to experience meaning in work regardless of whether the company
is selling insurance or building routers.

The character strengths are organized into six virtues: wisdom,
courage, humanity, justice, temperance, and transcendence. Peterson
and Seligman studied every culture and every religion throughout the ages
to come up with the six major virtues. You can take the assessment at
www.viacharacter.org and see what you think about the model and your
results.

The VIA character strengths are much closer to what *New York Times*
columnist David Brooks has recently called eulogy virtues rather than
résumé virtues.[16] Résumé virtues are the skills you bring to the business.
For instance, do you see opportunities, or know how to pull the levers to
make a business profitable? Eulogy virtues are deeper and the things
people will say about us when we die. You don't hear much at funerals
that could be put on the dead person's résumé. You hear a lot about
kindness, bravery, humor, and perspective at funerals. One of the

challenges of authentic leadership in business is to lead and promote both résumé and eulogy virtues, or in VIA terms, character strengths. You do not have to choose, but you do have to be clear about what eulogy virtues you hold dear. What would you want said about you at your funeral? Authentic leaders are clear about what is important from a character perspective. This requires self-examination and thought.

On a practical level, figuring out exactly what you hold dear and value is a first step toward deriving meaning from your work. Meaning is derived at work through the expression of your unique character. Character has two definitions. The first definition of character is the mental or moral qualities distinctive to an individual. Our moral qualities or values are unique to us as individuals, and as Peterson and Seligman have clarified, there are recurrent patterns throughout history regarding what humans find to be virtuous or meaningful.

The second definition of character also has relevance to the development of authentic leaders. A character is a person in a novel, play, or movie. Characters are developed or revealed in such great works. We must notice how we are developing over time and realize that what gives us meaning at one phase of our professional or personal lives may not give us meaning five years from now. The quest for meaning and purpose is a daily one and requires us to pay attention because meaning matters.

The baby boomers also set out to change the world in the 1960s. So, the Millennials and Gen Xers entering the workplace and expressing a desire to change the world is not really that shocking. Changing the world only happens when people are practicing their strengths of character. Looking for a way to change the world can actually be a cop-out and help you avoid figuring out how to be yourself. Doing the work of figuring out how to be yourself is much more achievable than an action plan to change the world.

It is easy to get caught up in thinking that you need to be Nelson Mandela, Gloria Steinem, or Martin Luther King, Jr. and change the world in order to have meaning in your work. One of my personal heroes of late is author and consultant Marie Kondo. Marie's work addresses the real problem in the developed world of people being overwhelmed by too much stuff. Her book titled *The Life-Changing Magic of Tidying Up* has been purchased by at least 2 million people globally.[17] She counsels people to get rid of objects that do not spark joy. To be sure, helping people get rid of clutter sounds less awe-inspiring and virtuous than ending apartheid. Most people are not aware that objects spark emotions and likely have not really thought about that. Her work enables people to get more done that matters in their lives because they are not distracted by clutter and therefore become more aware of their own emotions. That is practical, real-world value in the lives of people.

The Workouts

- Ask yourself the George Bailey questions cited at the beginning of this chapter next Tuesday. Write down your answers. What did you learn? Apply your learning in some way on Wednesday. It can be small. For example, one of my clients decided to not allow himself to use the mute button if he had a conference call. It kept him more engaged because he could not type or text other people if everyone was listening.

- Give the seven steps of authentic leadership development a try. Practice one new behavior. Again, think small. For example, if you usually talk too much, talk less. If you tend to hold back, speak up twice in your next meeting.

- Take the VIA strengths-finder assessment at www.viacharacter.org. It is available free of charge online. There is no catch. Figure out how you can use one of your character strengths more often in your current role. What would it look like to practice curiosity or another one of the 24 character strengths more often in your current role? Be careful, you may start to experience meaning that is self-determined!

3

TRUTH, LIES, AND AUTHENTICITY

"Our life is an apprenticeship to the truth that around every circle another can be drawn; that there is no end in nature, but every end is a beginning, and under every deep a lower deep opens."[1]

—Ralph Waldo Emerson

Allow me to be blunt: People lie. Leaders lie. Followers lie. You lie, and yes, I lie. Telling the whole truth and nothing but the truth is just not realistic or pragmatic. If your boss says to you: "I'm excited about having Bob move over to our team from supply chain. He brings a great skill set. Will you help him get to know the rest of the team?" You say, "Sure, no problem."

You've never liked Bob. You have no intention of helping him become a part of the team. He undermined you two years ago when you were up for a promotion. But you won't tell your boss that you can't stand Bob for personal reasons. Telling the truth just isn't practical in this case. Is it still possible for you to be authentic and be careful what you say to your boss?

Now for my most frequent type of lie. My smart friend asks, "Did you read the op-ed piece in *The New York Times* on Sunday about the crisis in Syria?" "Yes," I reply, "it was thoughtful." It is probably a reasonable bet to say it was thoughtful. The problem with my answer is the yes part. I have no idea what the op-ed regarding Syria said or did not say!

To use a phrase coined by Maria Sirois, we find ourselves in these moments "standing in a lie."[2] Most of us tell those little white lies and then move on quickly without any deep analysis. We don't usually take the time to stand in the lie. We keep moving mentally and physically. Standing in a lie means stopping in those everyday moments and considering the consequences to ourselves and others.

As Maria explains, we can choose to just move on without really experiencing the effect of our own lie on our hearts and minds. The alternative to just moving on is to stand consciously in the lie that you have just told. In order to stand consciously in your own lie, you have to slow down internally and admit it to yourself. You also have to become aware of your own thoughts and feelings about the lie. Paradoxically, practicing authenticity requires the acknowledgement of your falseness.

❧

SEEING THE MULTIPLE CHOICE QUESTIONS

Neither of the situations that I have just described seems that consequential when looked at in isolation. So you don't tell your boss that you won't help Bob. Big deal. Not helping Bob is one choice. Though the situation with Bob appears to be a yes or no situation, it's really a case of multiple choice.

You could help Bob or you could not help Bob—but you also have the choice to reevaluate your opinion of Bob. You don't really know all the pressures that Bob was under two years ago. You could choose to give Bob the benefit of the doubt. And look at your own life—you've probably learned and grown over the past two years. He might have changed and evolved as well. You also have the choice to overtly welcome Bob and watch him carefully at the same time. Remember the old adage *keep your friends close and your enemies closer*. The choices go on and on. You could also choose to say yes to helping and openly acknowledge that you have reservations about Bob.

In this less hierarchical digital age, most of us get caught up in our patterns and only see one or two choices when workplace situations are most often multiple choice. Practicing the art of authenticity in the real world requires us to see the multiple choices as opposed to being locked into an either-or reality. Jim Collins coined the phrase "the genius of the and" in 1994.[3] Collins argued that companies that are built to last do not get caught up in the "tyranny of the or" but lean into the "genius of the and." In order to practice the art of authenticity, you have to see the ands. When clients get caught up in either/or, black-and-white thinking, I irritate them by asking "what else?" They come up with something, then I say "what else?" If they are totally mystified and stuck in the either/or space, I will say I had a client who did not do either one of those in a similar situation. He did x.

As for my lie in which I present myself as the consummate intellectual who has read everything in *The New York Times,* you can look at that from a strict right/wrong point of view and say Karissa lied. That is wrong. Give her demerits. She is not authentic. But what is the rest of the story? How does my own lie impact me? As a result, do I continue to erect barriers that keep people from knowing and understanding me as I really am because of my need to appear like I have it all together? Is my need for people to view me as smart keeping people from really knowing me? Who is suffering as a result of that lie? Is it me, or the person I say that to?

The questions and issues that we must deal with in both our personal and work lives regarding truth, lies, and authenticity are rarely simple yes-or-no questions. The questions are multiple choice and often require an essay to navigate skillfully. In order to navigate skillfully, we have to embrace a bigger, broader, more pragmatic view of truth, lies, and authenticity. That is what this chapter is all about.

❧

KILLING THE DEAD BUG VIEW OF TRUTH

Authentic people tell the truth, the whole truth, and nothing but the truth. The fakers are the liars. If only it were that simple. We cannot separate the art and the science of authenticity from the gritty realities of truth and lies. However, the relationship is not as clear-cut as we would like to think. In our own minds, we are often operating with what Joseph Badaracco, Jr. of Harvard Business School refers to as "the dead bug view of truth" in situations that are actually far more complicated and consequential.[4] The dead bug view is straightforward and simple. You walk along and see a dead bug on the floor. You say the bug is dead. Or alternatively, you are walking along and your clothes are getting wet and drops are falling from the sky and you hear thunder. It is an easily observable fact that it is raining or that a bug is dead. Real-world dilemmas and interactions are not quite that simple.

If you were going to apply the dead bug view of truth to the situation described earlier with Bob joining your team, you would simply say to your boss: "I really don't want Bob on the team. I don't like him because he undermined me two years ago. So no, boss, I will not be welcoming him and/or easing his transition." We all know saying that to your boss in that situation is absurd and naive. However, most of us are not sure what else to do as we think about the relationship between truth and authenticity. We don't say that, but we also don't think too much about what we said or did not say either. The boss will likely forget anyway as he or she has a lot going on. So, we sweep that little day-to-day stuff under the rug and don't really think about it too much. We save up all our energy and genuine head-scratching for the big stuff.

For those on the path to authenticity, it is time to kill the dead bug view of truth and invest more energy in day-to-day choices. If you are careful in the small stuff and are tuning in to yourself, you are more likely to skillfully and authentically handle the big things, like whether to relate sensitive information to a friend who is about to be downsized. You have trained your brain to see the multiple choices and, as you will learn throughout the book, how your unique experiences affect the way you see everyday situations.

Countless times during the past 15 years, I have sat with a leader who had the unpleasant task of eliminating jobs. Often, that involves making and/or implementing a decision that will impact the lives of friends you have known for many years. I sat with one manager named Renee as she sorted through her own feelings about implementing a decision that would result in the loss of hundreds of jobs (on Good Friday of all days).

From her point of view, the decision was absolutely the right thing for the business, as new technology had essentially made several jobs unnecessary and the operation could function at much lower costs. However, a close friend she had known for more than 20 years would be out of a job within the next six months. Their families were close. She agonized over what it would be like to spend time with her friend over the next six months and be unable to discuss the situation.

The management committee had been clear that it was in the best interest of the entire organization not to discuss the layoffs until everything was finalized. The CEO had gone around the room and asked each individual if they could commit as an officer of the company to not discussing the issue with anyone outside that closed circle. From an ethical point of view, the expectation was clear that everyone who knew what was going to come down had to be silent until the formal announcement. How would Renee's friend feel when the news came down within the next six months? How would their relationship be impacted? Should she give her friend a heads-up? Her friend was obviously going to have an emotional reaction. Although she trusted her friend, could she trust him to be quiet if she did let him know?

Renee was in a bind between two deeply held personal values. She valued her role as an officer of her company and was loyal to the organization. She also had a great deal of respect and believed that the right thing to do for the good of the organization was to honor her word to her superiors and not tell her friend. In contrast, she also cared deeply about her friend and wanted to warn him. Her lifelong friend would be out of a job, which could affect his entire family—including his children who went to school with her children.

This type of dilemma is common and is indicative of what Joseph Badaracco called a choice between right and right. Bill George clarified the importance of authentic leaders doing the work to be in tune with their values and knowing their own personal true north.[5] In this case, Renee was well aware of her own values and was clearly a values-centered leader. She knew her true north. What tools are of use for authentic leaders in these right vs. right dilemmas?

The first step for authentic leaders in these messy situations is to sort out their own feelings. This sounds a lot easier than it actually is. With a little persistence, I can usually get my clients there. I start with innocuous questions like, "What is this like for you to know that your friend is going to lose her job?" Some of the feelings that managers have in these complicated situations are predictable, and we would hope that everyone would experience them. For example, we would hope that every manager would have some level of empathy for a friend who is losing a job. The particular flavor, tone, and intensity of that empathy varies from individual to individual. Many of the specific feelings below the surface level of analysis in these situations are idiosyncratic to the individual leader and are based on life experiences.

Boas Shamir and Galit Eilam from Hebrew University in Jerusalem argue that the essence of authentic leadership development is in the articulation of the leader's life story.[6] Foundational research has indicated that successful executives learn through experience.[7] Classic methodology involved qualitative interviews in which successful executives told stories in retrospect after they had already made it to the senior level. Through crafting their life stories, leaders come to a deeper understanding of what is meaningful and important to them. This exercise of crafting and making sense of one's experiences or story is ongoing, as one's story is ongoing and never static. If you're an American executive who successfully turns around a business with a diverse team in Europe, you return to the United States a different executive with an important new chapter in your story. Leadership development through understanding your story is highly personal, and not likely to happen in an intense weeklong off-site in which you take in a lot of information, including psychological data.

As an advisor, my role is to ignite authentic leadership development through bringing out the stories in the middle of the action and connecting the story to the here-and-now dilemmas. On a practical level, I am constantly getting my clients to tell me their stories. This is not like lying on a couch for psychoanalysis—though my clients do all like to joke about Freud and couches. That process of connecting the dots between who they are as unique individuals and the current situation is the essence of authentic leadership development.

In this case, I knew Renee well and had a few working hypotheses about what might be working her up in this situation that were unique to her. Renee's earliest ambitions in life had been toward helping others, and she currently served on countless nonprofit boards that served vulnerable people. As we talked, it became clear that the idea that a skillset was outdated struck her as making her friend particularly vulnerable and seemed unfair. She herself was first-generation college educated and was not a stranger to hard times. As we delved deeper, it became clear that she believed that if this could happen to her friend, it could also happen to her. And perhaps it could. All of these emotions were unique to Renee. Other clients from different backgrounds would have had a whole different collection of below-the-surface emotions.

The art of authenticity requires emotional archaeological digs that go below the pop psychology surface. In Renee's unique emotional calculus, not telling her friend somehow equated to not helping someone who was vulnerable. Not okay in the unique system of Renee's moral identity. Yet as an officer of the company, she could be fired on ethical grounds for giving her friend the heads-up. Welcome to the real world.

In our discussion, we began to explore how Renee could live out her value of helping vulnerable people in this situation. Renee was obsessively focused on getting through the next six months of family outings with her friend. I asked her a question that opened up a new frontier in our discussion: "What happens after the layoff?" Had the company discussed providing transition services and, if so, what kind? People are most vulnerable in the first six months after a layoff.

Ultimately, Renee took the lead in pushing for robust services to help people land on their feet after the layoff. She was successful in that quest and was deeply proud of her action. The next six months of interacting with her friend were not the easiest for Renee, but the friendship survived the layoff and Renee grew as an authentic leader. The action that she took in that situation is indicative of what I call the Reinhold Niebuhr rule. Reinhold Niebuhr was a twentieth-century American theologian often credited with the Serenity Prayer, which reads:

God grant me the serenity to accept the things I cannot change,

Courage to change the things I can,

And wisdom to know the difference.

Renee could not change the fact that shifts in the marketplace demanded layoffs. Nor could she change the fact that one of her oldest friends was caught in the vortex. However, she did have the power to impact the way the whole thing came down for everyone in the company, not just her friend. The company responded and provided help to former employees who were now vulnerable in a rough job market. For Renee, she was practicing authenticity and coming from her own values. Throughout the experience, Renee saw multiple choices and understood that being true to your values was not always about telling everything that you know. The dead bug view of truth was dead for Renee.

⟨◈⟩

Big Fat Whoppers and Sweet Little Lies

The notion of being honest is always linked with authenticity. It is seductive to do so and to think there are two types of people: authentic people with integrity and liars without integrity. However, both common sense and research have made it clear that lying is a part of everyday human interaction. Lying often functions as a kind of social lubricant. Too much truth can certainly disrupt the peace in everyday social interactions. In the 1997 movie *Liar Liar*, Jim Carrey portrays a duplicitous lawyer who is struck by a curse that has made it impossible for him to lie for 24 hours.[8] He speaks the whole truth and nothing but the truth for 24 hours. What would happen in your life at work or home if someone cast such a spell on you?

Leading social psychologist Bella DePaulo has been studying lying for more than three decades.[9] Her key findings include that we humans are quite aware of the lies that we are telling when we take the time to stop and think about them. DePaulo's pioneering studies in the 1990s required two separate groups to keep journals for a week and log every time they lied. One group consisted of college students, and the other group was a random sample from the community that varied in basic demographic variables such as age, income, and so on. The journals were confidential, and even the researchers knew the subjects only by assigned confidential numbers. The college students told two lies per day on average, and the group from the larger community told at least one lie per day on average.

DePaulo made it clear that average people in her studies, including the college students, do not typically feel good about their lies.

Most everyday lies fall into one of two categories. The first type of lie is called a self-centered lie, and those are the lies we tell to make ourselves look good. Even with self-centered lies, things are not always what they seem. A lie may not just be a lie. One of my recent clients named Catherine was really struggling with the workload in a new job. Her boss had a gut sense that something was wrong. He kept asking Catherine how her transition was going and if he could help. She repeatedly assured him that things were going well and that she was coming up to speed, when in fact she was drowning and beginning to miss deadlines. Her boss became increasingly frustrated with her unwillingness to admit that she was struggling. She was afraid to admit any weakness, and he was quickly losing faith in her ability to do the new job. Telling the lie to make herself look good was actually making her look bad.

My assignment was to assess Catherine and offer advice to her frustrated boss. Things were not nearly as bad as he had imagined. As I began to get to know her, I asked her to tell me about a time when she had helped someone else be successful. A lot of stories came out in response to that question. Then, I asked her to tell me about a time when someone else really helped her be successful. A blank look came across her face. She could not come up with a single time. She was in a highly technical area, and most of her assignments had been as an individual contributor. Even her preferred sports as a kid were primarily individual sports. She loved tennis and horseback riding and had excelled in both. It became clear in our conversation that in her mind, accepting her boss's help meant that she was not competent to do her job.

We all have our own meaning-making systems in our heads, and they are a part of our authentic selves. They are unique to us as individuals and are based in our backgrounds. Sometimes, they are productive and helpful and sometimes they're not.

Looking at Catherine's behavior in terms of absolute truths and lies, she was lying to her boss. But through self-exploration and figuring out that growth at this stage in her career meant learning to rely on others, she began to question and update her own meaning-making system. She ultimately was candid with her boss and said, "You're right, I am struggling. I want to get better at relying on other people to get things done so that I can be a more effective leader." This became a defining moment in which she learned how to operate more effectively at a higher level not in the abstract but in the real world. The deeper truth in her situation was that she needed to revise her view of what it meant to be competent in her new job. If her boss had decided that she was dishonest and played by the black-and-white rules, she would not have had the opportunity to learn and grow. She actually became more authentic in terms of having a higher level of real practical self-awareness.

The second most common type of lie according to DePaulo's research is an other-centered lie. These are the lies we tell to protect the feelings of someone else. In the workplace, these lies take many forms. One of the more common forms is soft-pedaling performance feedback.

Here is what happens in Act One of this typical workplace drama of duplicity. A manager calls me and says that one of his new direct reports named Thomas has awful communication skills. The manager attended Thomas's all-employee meeting the week before and felt appalled. The first thing I ask the manager is if he gave his new direct report feedback on this subject. The manager on the other end of the phone says, "Yes, and I told him I had a great resource for him named Karissa."

Act Two. I meet with Thomas, who has supposedly been told that his communication skills are awful. As we are getting acquainted, I begin to process that he has absolutely no idea why he is meeting with an organizational psychologist and is concerned that something is terribly wrong. His boss perceived that he had been clear and directly pointed out that Thomas's communication needed to improve drastically. I have often been tempted to ask for iPhone videos of these supposedly direct feedback meetings!

Regardless of what really happened, the message was not received. In the meeting with Thomas, I begin to adjust and ask more general questions and formulate a plan to salvage what could quickly turn into a train wreck of a meeting.

Act Three. I call the manager after the meeting and report that Thomas has no idea that his boss is really worried about his communication skills. The manager stammers and beats around the bush a bit. I cut to the chase and say we need to get Thomas accurate feedback.

Let's solve the problem. Do we need to do a formal 360? He says yes and we are off. Was the soft-pedaling manager inauthentic? He definitely told a lie. It became clear that he really was too concerned with Thomas's feelings to tell him the truth about his current level of communication skills. Is it simply a case of the soft-pedaling manager lacking courage? Was he duplicitous by nature? How could this situation be used to develop both the manager and Thomas as more authentic leaders?

Other insights from research on lying include that people clearly discriminate between sweet little lies and serious lies or big fat whoppers. Not surprisingly, people experience much more discomfort over the big fat whoppers like having an affair or lying about money. Some of the people who tell the big fat lies in business get caught and wind up on television. Those are dramatic events that stand out in our memories.

However, the interesting chapters in the development of the vast majority of authentic leaders are much more like the stories of Catherine and the soft-pedaling manager—everyday choices that set in motion relationships with other people that are more or less honest. How the manager in the above example views and relates to himself is also important in the development of authentic leaders. Authentic people are driven by autonomy, connectedness, and competence. Autonomy comes out in the need to express that you are unique and can accomplish things on your own, as in Catherine's story. Most of our lying at work and at home has to do with fear of loss of connection. It is not that we lie to disrespect people. We lie to protect ourselves from the rejection and disapproval of others. The soft-pedaling manager really valued Thomas and feared that giving him difficult feedback would ruin their relationship and Thomas would leave and go to another company.

The closer the relationship, the less likely people are to engage in small lies to make themselves look good. You know that you are building truly collaborative relationships when people begin to let you in on their shortcomings, such as a lack of PowerPoint skill or a bad sense of direction.

People are also much less likely to lie in person than on the phone. It really is more difficult to lie when you are literally looking at people. This has huge implications in our wired world. If we follow the logic of the research, the less distant the type of communication, the less likely we are to fudge the truth.

What impact do big fat whoppers, sweet little lies, and lies of omission have on leaders themselves? Renee's story indicates that not telling the truth to her friend was actually a growth experience for her as an authentic leader. Catherine also really grew from stepping up and telling her boss that she was feeling overwhelmed and really grew as a leader. The soft-pedaling manager's lie was actually motivated by a respect for his employee. We typically think of others as the victims of our lies, but research has made it clear that we are at least equally affected as well by our everyday lies. We know when we are lying. The practice of authenticity requires us to notice our lies and make sense of them. What motivated the lie? Is there a part of our story that needs a revision? Is there a value that we need to figure out how to put into practice in a really awful situation? Are we seeing things as a yes or no and missing the multiple choice questions?

THE TRUTH ABOUT AUTHENTICITY

The art of authenticity is the process of inventing yourself. It is an active process of experimentation and figuring things out. You trust what you know through your own experiences. Introspection deeper than the pop psychology level becomes a habit of mind. Central to the process of self-invention is the telling, revising, and understanding of your own life experiences and your story.

We use the term *invent* more often in relation to inventing a new machine or object. Gutenberg's invention of the printing press changed the world. So did the invention of Martin Luther King, Jr., courageous civil rights leader, by Martin Luther King, Jr. the man. He responded to the forces of history and invented himself, to use Warren Bennis's term. The principal definition of *invent* literally means to create or design something that has not existed before. You take all of the elements, including your history, thought patterns, emotions, values, and motivations, and combine them into an integrated, adaptable, whole operating system that is uniquely you. Authentic leaders are self-inventors. Warren Bennis wrote in his classic *On Becoming a Leader*: "Until you make your life your own, you're walking around in borrowed clothes. Leaders, whatever their field, are made up as much of their experiences as their skills, like everyone else. Unlike everyone else, they use their experience rather than being used by it. What distinguishes the leader from everyone else is that he or she takes all of that and creates a new, unique self."[10]

As we have discussed in this chapter, the practice of authenticity requires a willful, proactive struggle to behave in alignment with multiple and conflicting values. One of the bedrock values of authentic leaders is truth-seeking. Seeking the truth is a choice that one makes to face reality about oneself, one's situation, or one's business in as direct a manner as is possible. Truth-seeking is a bigger concept than honesty or lying. Leaders who are authentic and truth-seeking set up conditions for multiple and ongoing honest conversations. They pursue the goal of knowing and dealing in the truth with the awareness that there are always multiple sides of an issue and that it is not always easy to face situations head-on. Said in Emerson's more poetic terms, authentic leaders view themselves as being apprentices to the truth. Authentic action is intentional and carefully chosen to express what is most important or what is valuable in particular situations. Authenticity, in psychological terms, is not an either/or. Authenticity is a continuum, like most other psychological traits. Think about the more familiar introversion vs. extroversion. No one is purely introverted or extro-verted. No one is totally authentic or not.

Does authenticity work? Will being authentic make you a more effective leader in your world? Let me tell you a story about Domino's Pizza and a CEO named J. Patrick Doyle. *Wall Street Journal* reporter Stephen Moore visited Doyle at company headquarters in Ann Arbor, Michigan.[11] In Doyle's five years as CEO, annual sales have increased to $9 billion from $2 billion. In 2015, the stock price of Domino's hovers around $100, up from a low of $13 in 2010. Early on in his tenure, Doyle learned through focus groups that consumers thought the pizza tasted awful. His extraordinary out-of-the-box approach was to sign off on an ad campaign that showed consumers declaring that the pizza was awful. To top it all off, he appeared in each commercial and said, "We hear you, America. Give us another chance." Sales went through the roof as consumers gave Domino's another try. The cold, hard, unvarnished truth worked. Doyle is not following anyone else's playbook. He is a self-inventor and has reinvented the entire company.

The relationship between truth, lies, and authenticity is not a straightforward, linear path of clear rules. You have to be willing to adapt and build your own playbook like J. Patrick Doyle. To be sure, it is not always as easy to link the truth or the lie as directly to the success or failure as in the Domino's story.

In aggregate, simple choices and habits shape who we are becoming. Are we becoming more or less authentic? Our choices about telling the truth, outright lying, or fudging the truth affect not just other people. Our choices deeply affect us and are the turning points in our stories. Our choices to accept the ambiguity and complexity inherent in the messy world of leading and making decisions—and not settling for the easiest, least painful course of action—are what define us. All of our choices determine whether we are inventing ourselves and being authentic or going with the flow and not having the courage to figure out and express who we are and who we are becoming. The process of becoming more authentic amid the pressures of everyday organizational life and life in general requires inquiry, deep introspection, and most important, placing a value on self-invention.

⎯⎯⎯✥⎯⎯⎯

THE WORKOUTS

- Think of someone you know and really respect as a leader. In this experiment, you get to do what I get to do every day! Ask them the following question: "When you think about the process of becoming the leader that you are today, what experiences stand out for you as turning points?" Listen carefully.

- Go on a multiple choice expedition next Thursday. Identify three situations that you would normally see as simple yes-or-no situations and reframe them as multiple choice issues. They can be important or simple. "Shall I go to the gym or not" could turn into shall I:

  a. go to the gym

  b. avoid exercising at all costs

c. go to the movies

d. take a walk

e. both c and d

- Keep a log of your lies for a week just as the participants in DePaulo's original study did. Keep a journal and write down every lie that you tell with a brief description of the situation. Are you above average in your frequency? Do you most often tell lies to protect yourself, or are most of your lies other-centered?

PART II

THE SCIENCE OF AUTHENTICITY

4

FOLLOWERS BEWARE . . . OF CHARISMA

"Men are so simple of mind, and so much dominated by their immediate needs, that a deceitful man will always find plenty who are ready to be deceived."

—Niccoló Machiavelli, *The Prince*[1]

He's not who I thought he was," she said. I had just joined a former client for lunch at a hip sushi joint in New York. "I was so excited to come to work at this company but mostly to come to work with and for Charlie. He seemed so bright and so interested in having me join his team."

We ordered drinks and she continued: "I felt on top of the world when I took this job. It is hard to believe that I have only been working here a year. Within the first month, I started to figure out that things were a little off. My bonus did not turn out exactly as it was promised when I looked at the paperwork in detail. Then, a colleague left and I picked up her work—temporarily, I thought. I still have her work and my work. The morale of the team gets worse every month. I have tried to address issues with Charlie, but I just leave his office either convinced it is only me or that he is really trying to make things work. He seems to dodge negative feedback like a superhero deflecting bullets. How could I have been this wrong about a person? I left a job I loved to come here and follow a fake, an imposter."

By the time the waitress impatiently looked at us as if to say *Are you going to order yet?* my client was in tears.

My client is asking herself some tough questions. We have all been there. We believed in someone, followed them, and they did not turn out to be who we thought they were. We felt deceived. We felt stupid. How could we have been so wrong?

This chapter is the "follower beware" chapter. If you are serious about being an authentic leader, you need to follow other authentic leaders. There are bad guys out there. There are people who are up to no good and who will tear you down no matter what you do. In these cases, it's not about you. You must accept that and be alert.

By the time you are in the workplace for 10 years, you will have encountered some of the bad guys and been burned. How can you be a bit wiser in your choices of whom to follow? The key, as in most things, is to learn from your mistakes. The goal of this chapter is to help you make sense of the mistakes you may have already made as well as help you avoid mistakes in the future. You will learn to use questions as tools and to carefully observe leadership behavior with a curious, open mind. If you don't feel comfortable asking some of the questions offered in the chapter at an appropriate time, that too can serve as a signal. Beware, you may be dealing with someone who is just not who he presents himself to be.

THE PERCEIVED POWER OF CHARISMA

More times than not in those situations, we have been blinded by the effects of charisma. Charismatic people are those people who excite us. They draw others into their orbit. We as followers get emotionally excited and may skip asking the probing questions or looking for the rest of the story. A charismatic leader appears to create a climate in which people can and do move metaphorical mountains in terms of creating new products or turning around a business. For example, both Jack Welch and Steve Jobs have delivered extraordinary results over a long period of time, and popular opinion would describe both as charismatic. Both Jobs and Welch have also been on the covers of every business magazine and have become celebrities in their own right, like Taylor Swift and Bono.

How much of their business success was due to charisma? We assume that their charisma was one of the keys to the phenomenal success of their companies. That intuitively makes sense. It is also hard to miss charisma. Here is what happens in our minds. We see two facts: The leader is charismatic and the company is successful. The two things are both happening so we tend to assume a connection. However, as I learned in my first research methods class, correlation does not equal causation. Just because two things are happening at the same time does not mean that one of them caused the other.

Business outcomes in particular are hard to link directly to leadership behaviors. Huge factors like what is going on in terms of the overall economic environment and the relevance of your product or service to what is happening at that moment in history all come into play. The role of charisma in leadership success is far from clear when we dig into the evidence.

In the '80s and early '90s, everyday people could not even name the CEOs of Fortune 100 companies. Celebrities were mostly entertainers. Things are different now. Business leaders are public figures, and the perceived power of charisma has escalated. But when we subject the importance of charisma in leadership effectiveness to rigorous investigation, we see a mixed bag at best. Highly successful leaders may or may not be charismatic. But it is easy to assume that charisma is more important than it is in this visual, digital era.

So we can't assume that charisma causes success. How does charisma relate to authenticity? People follow people they perceive to be authentic. However, sometimes those perceptions of authenticity change over time, and we see, just as my client did, that people are not who we thought they were. They reveal themselves over time, and we have all been deceived. Often, the leader's personal charisma has masked character flaws that could have been seen if we had investigated further.

Here comes the tricky part. Authentic leaders are not necessarily charismatic. Charismatic leaders are not necessarily authentic. Charisma can help leaders accomplish great things. But it's also true that leaders who lack charisma accomplish great things every day. In the United States, we tend to give too much credence to charisma. We love a good show. We enjoy the charismatic leader and are always fascinated with an interesting character who makes us feel positive emotions.

There is no conclusive research that tells us that charismatic leaders are more effective than noncharismatic leaders. To the contrary, Jim Collins described Level 5 leaders in his influential text *Good to Great*[2] as humble and hard working. His study of CEOs who successfully transitioned a company from mediocrity to greatness did not find that the charisma of the leader really mattered. This point of view was confirmed in Collins's most recent study, fully explained in *Great By Choice*.[3] He compared companies that thrived under unfavorable and ambiguous market conditions with their competitors in the same space who did not thrive. Charisma was not found to be a differentiating leadership behavior. Across the companies that thrived, the consistent leadership behaviors were fanatic discipline, productive paranoia, and empirical creativity. These factors are far less sexy than charisma. I have never had a client get overexcited about a potential boss's discipline, paranoia, or empirical creativity!

The word *charisma* has roots in ancient biblical texts with multiple references in the old and new testaments. The root word of *charisma* means divine, extraordinary, or like the gods. Max Weber, the influential German sociologist, was the first to bring the idea of charisma into the discussion regarding human behavior in social groups with his foundational text titled *The Theory of Social and Economic Organization*.[4] Weber saw charisma as a special personality characteristic that made certain people extraordinary, and those charismatic people were able to change the world for the better. In his view, charismatic people have exceptional powers and should be revered. The evidence of charisma was that followers were loyal and revered the leader. This early twentieth-century view still affects us today.

I often find that my normal clients with great qualities like fanatic discipline who are accomplished accountants, engineers, and attorneys become overwhelmed when they think of becoming a great leader. They assume that being a great leader requires a huge presence and an ability to draw people like a magnet. They are confusing great leadership with charisma. We have all seen too many films of Martin Luther King, Jr. and John F. Kennedy. King's "I Have a Dream" speech and Kennedy's audacious promise that we would take a man to the moon and return him safely are extraordinary moments in American history. However, we have talked about the charismatic side of leadership and the big moments way too much in our attempts to develop leadership in the classroom. Being an authentic leader requires a daily, consistent discipline that could very well look boring at times. Neither King nor Kennedy maintained such a powerful presence all of the time. Both of them got up every morning and stumbled around like the rest of us.

⹂⹃

TWO FLAVORS OF CHARISMA

Charisma can have a dark side, as both Adolf Hitler and Osama bin Laden could be described as charismatic according to Weber's definition. Remember, according to Weber, the evidence of charismatic leadership was possessing devoted followers. It is rather ironic that 70 years later we have metrics to measure followers with our digital media tools such as Twitter and Facebook. What would Max Weber say about that? In order to gain insight, current social science research examines the dynamics among a leader's followers. In other words, emphasis is placed on how the followers interact with one another, not just how they view and interact with the leader.

As you will learn in this section, it is important to ask several questions about the dynamics among a leader's followers. Robert House and Jane Howell[5] distinguished between two types of charismatic leadership. They called one type of charismatic leadership "socialized" and the other type "personalized." We will call these two flavors or types of charismatic leadership the *greater good* (GG) vs. *greater me* (GM). The

GG charismatic leaders lead the overall enterprise, the collective, toward a better future. The GM leaders may be using the same language as the GG leaders, but their motives are very different. GM leaders generally move toward enhancing themselves, at the expense of the collective if necessary.

Detecting and understanding the motives of others is nearly impossible. Understanding our own motives can be challenging enough. Real people are not pure GG or pure GM leaders. Leaders are like all real people. We are all a mix of looking out for ourselves and looking out for others and the overall good of the collective. Some leaders may be 90 percent looking out for the greater good and 10 percent greater me. Others may be 80/20 in the other direction. You can see there's an infinite number of hybrid possibilities. Given all of this complexity, how do we make use of the distinction between the two types of charismatic leaders?

Social scientists Paul Varella, Mansour Javidan, and David Waldman[6] took a stab in a thought-provoking academic paper. They started with the following working hypothesis: The impact of socialized (GG) charismatic leadership on the ways in which people interact with one another is very different from the way in which personalized (GM) charismatic leadership impacts interactions on work groups. So instead of looking at how charismatic leadership impacts followers one-on-one, the authors strived to apply a broader lens and study how charismatic leaders impact the ways in which all of the followers relate to one another. Simply put, what kinds of team and interpersonal interactions and overall tone do these two types of charismatic leaders impact among all of their followers?

The authors identified three personal qualities of all charismatic leaders and then differentiated between GG and GM leaders, based on how all of those qualities played out in the group level of analysis. Three personal qualities shared by all charismatic leaders are persuasive visionary communication, clear read of the overall situation, and self-confidence.

Both types of charismatic leaders communicated vision in a persuasive way. However, GG leaders were more likely to involve people in crafting the vision. People on the team actually related and owned the vision as is evidenced by consistent referencing of the ideas in the vision. Individuals have different takes on why different parts of the vision really matter. In contrast, teams who followed a GM leader reference the leader more than the ideas.

In my own client work, I've seen this play out. One executive team that I worked with mentioned the name of their leader (who was not present) 88 times in a 90-minute meeting. So the tip here is to notice how often the team mentions and invokes the name of the leader vs. addressing the ideas, and more important how to realize the vision in their conversation.

The second quality that all charismatic leaders of both types possess is a clear read of the overall situation. Leaders in business are constantly reading the external environment (or marketplace) and how well the internal organization is equipped to be successful in the marketplace. GM leaders tend to emphasize an "us vs. them" mentality in regard to competitors. Hence, GM leaders are more threat based in the way they talk about business issues. GG leaders are more inclined to view difficulties in the marketplace as challenges in which the overall enterprise can become stronger.

Let's look at an example to make sense of this. Imagine a small town that has two primary car dealerships. For decades, the town has had a Ford dealership and a Toyota dealership. All of a sudden, a Mercedes dealer has come into town. According to this theory, a GM leader would rally the troops to prevail against the new Mercedes dealer, the overt threat. A GG leader would approach it in a different manner. A GG leader would be more likely to emphasize things like how to use the event of the newcomer in the marketplace as a catalyst to improve the way their organization serves customers. The emphasis would be on strengthening the business to deal with the threat as opposed to the threat itself.

The third quality is self-confidence. We all display confidence or the lack thereof in a myriad of ways. Our sense of self-esteem is the backstage side of the way we humans display confidence. In other words, if we are confident externally, we experience higher self-esteem in our own heads and hearts. However, self-esteem can be high and fragile or high and stable.[7] If people have high, stable self-esteem, challenges come from the situation or from other people and internal self-esteem is not affected by those challenges. In contrast, those with high, fragile self-esteem are thrown off by those who challenge and disagree with them.

In practical situations, leaders who display very controlling behaviors are often acting out of a need to protect their fragile self-esteem. As long as they can control things, they can maintain their fragile but high sense of self-esteem. GG leaders actually invite disagreement and alternative views. Alternative views are not a challenge to their self-esteem. In contrast, GM leaders are more apt to shut down challenges to their thought process and promote one view exclusively, which is usually their own or one that makes them comfortable. In the real world, this plays out in hiring decisions. GM leaders tend to hire and surround themselves with people who are less experienced and won't ever be capable of assuming their role. GG leaders tend to hire and surround themselves with people who are as smart as or smarter than they are.

In summary, charismatic leaders vary in their emphasis toward the greater good or their emphasis toward the greater me, or self-enhancement. To be sure, both types of charismatic leadership can look the same. However, a clever follower should be alert to three things. First, how exactly does the leader's self-confidence play out in terms of whom he or she surrounds him- or herself with? Second, you should also be alert to how much the ideas in the vision are referenced vs. the "visionary" leader. Finally, notice how your leader talks about threats and challenges. Subtle differences in language can be clues to significant differences in the leader's internal wiring. Listening carefully to those subtle differences will decrease the probability of getting taken in by a GM boss.

Now, we will move on to the use of questions as powerful tools. If you really want to understand another person, you have be skillful enough to have conversations that matter. There is no better way to protect yourself than by really understanding your boss and your colleagues at a deeper level.

CONVERSATIONS THAT MATTER

I always get nervous when one of my clients gets super excited about an opportunity to work with a potential boss. There is one clue that

I am looking for, and if I see it, I ask questions that are no fun for me to ask and no fun for the client to answer, in order to burst their bubble and help them see things more clearly. The clue is if the client does not see any weaknesses in a potential boss. If the client cannot see any potential downsides in the boss or in working for the boss, the client has not been thinking clearly and is being driven by excitement.

There are no perfect bosses. You know how this goes. You are really excited about an opportunity and you just "clicked" with a potential boss. You left the meeting feeling on top of the world. You are impressed with that person's knowledge, sense of humor, and overall presence and energy. You are just wowed.

These situations always remind me of the early stages of romantic love, long before "he won't pick up his shoes." Over time, you come to realize that the boss you were so excited about working for took credit for one of your best ideas, or pushed you to hire someone you did not want to hire. This boss is not necessarily a GM leader or even a bad boss, just not the perfect boss.

These situations are not romantic, and the next phase of your career could be damaged by going to work for the wrong person. It is not always easy to break up with a boss and move on. Seeing your boss and other people as clearly as possible is the best defense and offense in the world of work. If you can't see any weakness or potential downside with a boss, you are not seeing the person clearly yet. You must ask questions, listen carefully, and observe, as opposed to just being wowed and being certain that this will be the best boss ever.

In this section, I cover specific questions and methods of focused behavioral observation. Both the questions and observational methods are designed to help you start conversations that matter. Use your curiosity to have conversations that go below the level of superficial chitchat, which can help you avoid following the wrong leader. Having honest conversations that matter will also make *you* a more authentic leader. This notion of starting conversations that matter is from the work of the influential leadership and systems theorist Margaret Wheatley. Here is an excerpt from her 2002 poem titled "Turning to One Another"[8] that captures the intention and approach to interacting with others that will help you become a more authentic leader as well as avoid following the wrong leaders.

Be brave enough to start a conversation that matters.

Talk to people you know.

Talk to people you never talk to.

Be intrigued by the differences that you hear.

Expect to be surprised.

Treasure curiosity more than certainty.

How many conversations have you had in the last week that were memorable? How many have you had that you can even remember? It is easy to go through your workday on autopilot and discuss the weather, the bad food, or what event your kids are going to over the weekend. There is absolutely nothing wrong with polite chitchat. It has its place. We must also make room in our lives for real conversations that matter. If you desire to be an authentic leader and to follow other authentic leaders, you must be brave enough to start such conversations. Conversations that matter go below the surface of things. We run the risk of being surprised. These conversations take energy and attention, and are also the only way to create substantive relationships in the workplace.

Here is an example. I was conducting an offsite with a team of high-performing manufacturing leaders. Their then-new president is an extreme athlete in his post-40 life and had been a hero on the battlefield in his youth. He strikes quite an intimidating figure and is smart as a whip. He is a man of few words, a man of substance, and few would describe him as overtly charismatic. He is the kind of guy who grows on you.

Presession interviews with the team revealed that they were struggling with his leadership and did not know where he was coming from. He decided to be brave enough to have a conversation that mattered with the entire team during the meeting. He opened up with the fact that the interpersonal side of leadership had always been difficult for him as he was more comfortable with ideas and numbers. Then he said: "I want us to figure out how to work together more effectively during the next few days. I know I am better at one-on-one conversations than talking in a group like this. So, I know that in order to be the most effective team that we can possibly be, I need to spend time regularly with all of you one-on-one. There has been a lot of stuff pulling me away from our one-on-one meetings. I am in control of my calendar so that is going to change. But what can we all do? I can't figure this out by myself. What changes do we need to make in order to be a more effective team?"

Wow. Not one person checked their e-mail as he offered that opening soliloquy. In response, everyone opened up, participated heartily, and committed to a change in behavior that they perceived would help make the overall team more effective. He had started a two-day conversation that mattered and ultimately changed the team dynamics.

You don't have to be at an offsite and it does not have to be a special occasion to have conversations that matter. You can create meaningful conversations as you go about your daily routine. If you are alert, opportunities emerge for you to have real conversations instead of staying on the surface of things. Questions are powerful tools if you want to start conversations that matter. Ultimately, develop your own set of questions that you feel comfortable with. As a start, I recommend that all of my clients become proficient in asking the following 10 conversational questions:

- Where are you from originally?
- What do you like to do in your spare time?
- What was your first leadership role?
- How do you choose people to hire for your team?
- What kinds of behaviors irritate you in colleagues?
- Whom do you admire?
- How would you describe yourself as a leader?
- What kinds of situations bring out the best in you?
- What kinds of situations bring out the worst in you?
- What is the hardest thing you have ever done as a leader?

The first question is generally nonthreatening and appropriate in almost any situation. I am often amazed, though, by how few people can tell me where their boss is originally from, or the colleagues they interact with every day. Sometimes the opposite of the perfect boss syndrome is going on and the client thinks the boss is just awful; in that case, the client can rarely tell me very basic stuff about the boss as a person, like where he or she is from. Certainty has taken hold; the client believes the boss is terrible, period, so why invest time and energy in learning more? That is true of all of us when we are not "clicking" with someone; we think we know who he or she is and stop being curious. Our view hardens. What can we possibly learn about people by asking where they are from, anyway?

The importance of early experience in shaping who we are is a well-accepted fact. After the person responds, try adopting a curious tone and ask what was it like to grow up in Minneapolis? Listen carefully and let your curiosity drive. Listen for whether a person grew up in a rural or urban area, what the culture was like, whether they ever go back, and what their early education was like. With this simple question, you can begin to understand how a person became who they are now.

"What do you do in your spare time?" Again, a really nonthreatening question. Does a person engage in a competitive sport, or do they love to travel to remote locations? Again, you are getting a sense of a whole person instead of just seeing one aspect of a person who shows up to a meeting at work and needs to move a project along. If they love golf, let your curiosity drive and ask for their handicap. Some people will answer with a number and a sense of pride. Others will laugh. Golf is an interesting one, as the interest can be primarily about pursuing excellence and mastering the game, or it can be primarily social, depending on the person. You can't put all golfers in the same category. This is where listening carefully is important, not just to the facts but the emotion, tone, and body language as well. Does the person become more animated when talking about this hobby?

"What was your first leadership role?" I use this one at team-building sessions all the time. It is generally nonthreatening, as I have never had anyone uncomfortable with it, and I have asked it in several groups larger than 15. People always see their colleagues a shade differently when they talk about being captain of the football team or working at the Safeway at the age of 16. This question helps people tune in to how others have evolved over time. It also can give you a sense of what they think is important in leading others. Do they focus on the results? Do they focus on their own performance? Do they focus on how they wound up in the leadership role? Did they like their first leadership role?

When I use this with executive groups, I do it in the following sequence. First, I ask them to describe their first leadership role in a short paragraph. Then, I ask them to write down the name of everyone else on the team on the same sheet of paper. They are to leave space after each name for a paragraph. Then, I say the most important aspect of the exercise is listening. Each of you will share what you wrote about your first leadership experience and we can all ask questions. Your assignment is to learn something new about each of your colleagues and write your learning down in the space you left after that person's name. The heart of the exercise is what you can learn about others, not yourself. This almost always warms up even the most difficult executive group. They typically take on the challenge to learn something new about each of their colleagues with a competitive tone, as in, "I am going to be the best at this exercise."

As they go from person to person, the tone shifts and they start having conversations that matter. This question, even though generally nonthreatening, is a deeper question than the first two. If someone starts talking about themselves and going through every role they have ever had, pay attention. They could be a GM leader or they could just like to talk a lot. Again, be curious and notice how individuals respond to the prompt of this interesting question.

"How do you choose people to hire for your team?" This one is more complicated than it appears. Whether or not your boss has thought a lot about this one is revealing. As you begin to experiment with this one, you will notice a lot of variation. Some bosses will give you pat answers like "I look for hard workers" and almost recite a formula. That can mean that they really don't know how they decide, or it could be a cover. For example, the pat answers could be a cover for "I hire people who make me feel good." (Remember those GM bosses we discussed earlier in the chapter.) Other people will say it depends or has changed a lot in the last few years. Still others will tell you stories about bad hires and good hires. Listen carefully and be curious. The person is giving you clues about who they really are.

"What kinds of behaviors irritate you or bother you?" Timing really matters on this one. It needs to be asked in the right situation. You can't just walk up to your boss at the mingle function and say, "Hey, what kinds of behaviors really irritate or bother you?" That is just awkward. It can be artfully used when you are struggling with another team member, though.

Imagine this scenario: You are in charge of pulling together the agenda for the monthly staff meeting. Two days before the meeting, your boss asks for the agenda. You say you're still waiting for input from the marketing lead named Ron. Your boss comments that this seems to be a monthly event and you confirm that, yes, it is an ongoing issue with Ron. You go on to say that you usually have to physically go over to the next building to get his input on anything. Then, you can ask how your boss would deal with this behavior if Ron were a peer. You can very easily segue into a conversation about what drives your boss crazy in colleagues. This question is really about self-knowledge. It can come out in a lot of different ways, but ultimately, knowing what kinds of behaviors drive you crazy is a key element of self-knowledge.

This one also requires more self-disclosure from your boss than the earlier questions. Does your boss seem comfortable with that level of self-disclosure, or try to change the subject? If you find it difficult to get your boss to have a conversation beyond the superficial, that is a sign. You may be dealing with someone who is not who he appears to be on the surface. Beware and keep noticing. With some people, it just takes time for them to open up. With others, it is never going to happen.

A question like "Whom do you admire?" gets at who your boss really wants to be. Think about the people you admire. You probably notice they all have qualities you would like to possess. They may also have qualities you detest. But we all admire specific people because of specific qualities. I tend to admire people who have a great breadth of intelligence and are deeply knowledgeable about a wide range of subjects. I can excuse a lot if I find a person to be intellectually interesting. What does that tell you about me? It is potentially telling you a lot about me if you are listening carefully. If I were your boss, you might make sure to present the broader picture to me on a regular basis. You might also hypothesize that I could be blind to the faults of certain people on the team who had a lot of intellectual horsepower. Notice the word *hypothesize*. In using questions to learn about your boss or colleagues, you are always listening carefully and forming working hypotheses, which can change in light of new evidence. Remember, curiosity is key. By allowing people to reveal themselves, you're less likely to become locked into a position of certainty.

"How would you describe yourself as a leader?" is a significant leap in depth from the earlier questions. Again, timing is crucial. This one is a good fit for a nontask situation and particularly a good fit for coaching and development conversations. A softer form of this one is "how would you like other people to describe you as a leader?" This one is quite popular these days, as most people are talking about their leadership brand in one shape, form, or fashion. Often, my clients tee up the original question or the softer form by referencing a leadership book they have just read. This question begins to get at core values.

Now, clever bosses who are good at selling themselves may nail this question and say something that sounds just right. Does it sound too right? Too neat and tidy? Does it come across as genuine? What nonverbal signals are you receiving as your boss answers this question? Does your boss mention any weaknesses? If not, you could hypothesize that he or she is not aware of any weaknesses, or does not feel comfortable throwing them on the table, or both. Continue to watch and learn about your boss or colleague.

The next two questions go together. Asking "What kinds of situations bring out the best in you?" and "What kinds of situations bring out the worst in you?" can help you learn how aware your boss is of how situations impact his or her behavior.

The *fundamental attribution error* is one of the most well-researched and consistent insights within social psychology. The fundamental attribution error is that behavior is heavily influenced by the pressures and forces inherent in situations. Situations impact behavioral choice as much as, or more than, personality drivers. The error is that we humans tend to overestimate the influence of personality and underestimate the influence of situational factors, especially when we are trying to make sense of the behaviors of others.

Don't expect your boss to lecture you on the fundamental attribution error! But notice your boss's level of awareness regarding how his or her behavior varies across situations. At a basic level, does your boss understand that he or she behaves differently across situations? Is your boss uncomfortable with the fact that his or her behavior varies? These two questions allow you to get a sense of your boss's depth and psychological complexity—or lack thereof.

Also think through how often you have witnessed variations in your boss's behavior across situations. *Machiavellian personalities* were identified by psychologist Richard Christie and Florence Geis.[9] These complex personalities were named after Machiavelli, who worked in the great courts of Florence during the Renaissance as an advisor to the leaders who ruled the world at that time. In essence, Machiavellian personalities are manipulative and willing to be deceitful to get their way.

The bosses to watch out for are referred to in the social sciences as "high Machs." There is a strong possibility that one of the bosses you have been deceived by in the past was a high Mach. High Machs have a vast ability to change their behavior in drastic ways across situations in order to get what they want. We all have to adapt to circumstances every day in the workplace, but high Machs may or may not be aware of the drastic shifts they make to accommodate to circumstances.

Back to curiosity in terms of the way your boss answers the question. No final diagnosis allowed. Does your boss avoid the question? How does the response to these questions fit with your observations? If you have a working hypothesis that your boss may be manipulative or Machiavellian, put your guard up. Watch out and watch your boss's behavior carefully. Do not be naive.

The tenth question is the power question: "What is the hardest thing you have ever done as a leader?" This question gets at what Bill George[10] called the *leadership development crucible*. Crucibles are vessels used in labs to expose chemical substances to heat, usually a Bunsen burner. Translating the metaphor to authentic leadership development, what happens to a person when they are under pressure and in a very difficult situation? In my world, we refer to these tests of leadership as having developmental heat.

These crucibles in leadership development can take many forms. They can be international assignments, unexpected downturns in the business, being tasked to turn around a failing business, making a judgment call to close down a plant, and/or leading a team that does not want to be led by you. This question asks about your boss's most difficult crucible.

Timing of this question is crucial. It is also important that you've been building a deeper relationship with your boss before you throw this one out. If you can't get engagement on some of the earlier questions, asking this one is probably ill advised. But if you have been working at this relationship and feel you are getting a sense of who your boss is beyond the surface, go for it and listen carefully and with curiosity to the answer.

People typically respond to this power question in one of three ways. Some people deflect it totally. Others will answer the question, and it will be clear they got through it and don't want to dwell on it or talk about it a lot. The third group will tell you the story and explain what they learned as a result of the experience. Bill George of the Harvard Business School teaches that navigating these crucibles and integrating the learning into who you are is one of the hallmarks of authentic leaders.

THE AUTHENTICITY CONTINUUM

We've covered a lot of ground in this chapter. As you pay more attention to the behaviors of your boss and yourself, do not neglect the obvious. Is your boss committed to being an authentic leader? Is it something your boss really cares about and demonstrates in language and behavior? If being authentic really matters to you or your boss, then you can become more authentic. Being authentic is not something you are or are not. It's not like being pregnant. If you listen to most casual conversations at work, we tend to assume that someone is either authentic or not. However, the notion of becoming more authentic is more accurate than any absolute dichotomy. Human beings are far too complex for absolute dichotomies.

Stanford psychologist Carol Dweck[11] delineated between the fixed mind-set and the growth mind-set. The fixed mind-set is just what it sounds like. You are either intelligent, or a good tennis player, or a good student, or not. It is fixed and based on your native abilities. People with a growth mind-set believe that with work they can become more authentic, more intelligent, and better tennis players. Guess which mind-set tends to lead to more success and higher levels of self-esteem. You got it, it's the growth mind-set. Think about authenticity as a continuum with an infinite number of places between being authentic and being a fake. Authentic leaders are seeking ways to become more authentic. Apply a growth mind-set in your thinking about authentic leadership, imagine that continuum, and be careful who you follow. There are bad actors out there who are not trying to become more authentic. You will be deceived again. There is no way to accurately read everyone. However, you are better equipped to avoid following the wrong people and to learn from your mistakes if you make regular use of the concepts and questions in this chapter as tools.

THE WORKOUTS

- The idea of asking probing questions is not new. One of the more fun ways to play with questions is the Proust Questionnaire.[12] There are several versions of the Proust questionnaire in circulation. The questions were used as a parlor game in Paris in the 1880s. Marcel Proust was a French novelist and the questions were popular in his social circle. The questions are light in tone but pull out interesting aspects of people. Answer the following questions for yourself and begin experimenting with one question that you like with others. Be careful with timing—and I am not necessarily recommending these as tools to get to know your boss!

What is your idea of perfect happiness?

What historical figure do you most identify with?

What is the trait you most deplore in yourself?

What do you consider the most overrated virtue?

Which talent would you most like to have?

If you were to die and come back as a person or a thing, whom or what do you think you would be?

What is your most treasured possession?

What is your motto?

- Pick out one of the recommended questions for your boss and find a way to ask it at the first opportunity. Listen carefully. Ask the question whether you like your boss or not. Learning more about your boss could change your view. Avoid those fixed mind-sets unless absolutely necessary.

- We talked in the chapter about greater good (GG) vs. greater me (GM) leadership. Remember that the vast majority of us are actually a mixed bag in that we look out for ourselves and for the greater good. It is not smart to be 100 percent looking out for the greater good, as others will take advantage of you. Really think about your own behavior. How would you characterize yourself? Are you 80 percent GG and 20 percent GM or the reverse? Are you satisfied with your current percentages? Would you like to change the ratio?

5

SELF-AWARENESS OR IS IT SELVES AWARENESS?

"We define authenticity as the unobstructed operation of one's true or core self in one's daily enterprise. However, instead of viewing authenticity as a single unitary process, we suggest that authenticity can be broken down into four separate, but interrelated components."
—Michael Kernis and Brian Goldman[1]

T he way we use the notion of self-awareness in business is incomplete. You will learn exactly what critical pieces are missing in this chapter and come away equipped with understanding to help you become both more authentic and effective. The concept of selves awareness encompasses all of the ways that you are like all other people, like some other people, and like no other person.

You are also entering the section of the book in which we dig into the key learnings from research in psychology for insight on how to become more authentic instead of less authentic as we grow across the lifespan.

Becoming more authentic will not happen naturally or without effort and intention. We all face both internal and external barriers as we seek to express our authenticity. Organizations of all kinds exert pressures to behave in very specific ways. That is what makes an organization efficient. The internal barriers that keep us from being more authentic are usually rooted in our unique histories. Being authentic as a leader requires a commitment to being proactive and creating your own work life. The relevant research on authenticity stems from the tradition of the humanistic psychologists, which asserts that people have a strong drive toward self-expression and determination that can become obstructed through life experiences. Becoming more authentic requires tapping into that innate drive toward self-determination and expression. For some of us, it is a process of rediscovery.

It has been validated by multiple researchers that authenticity is not just one thing. In research jargon, authenticity is a multiple-component variable. The development of psychological authenticity consists of four interrelated processes that require significant thought and attention from you. The work of Michael Kernis and Brian Goldman clarified that psychological authenticity consisted of four interrelated processes: awareness, unbiased processing, behavior, and relational orientation. In 2008, Walumbwa, Avolio, Gardner, Wernsing, and Peterson[2] built on the work on Kernis and Goldman and validated a multiple-component model of authenticity as it applied to leadership. They refined the language of the four components and used the following terms: self-awareness, balanced processing, relational transparency, and an internalized moral perspective. During the next four chapters, we will explore how to work on each of these components and become a more authentic leader. We will take the ideas from the ivory tower to the workplace of the twenty-first century. And selves awareness is the most fundamental of all the components.

SELVES AWARENESS AND THE CASE OF THE BOSSY CFO

We talk a lot about self-awareness as if there is one uniform self out there that is consistent day in and day out. Get that self figured out, know it, check the box and *voilà,* you have achieved self-awareness. That is just not very practical and it is certainly not grounded in what we understand about human beings as psychologists. The check-the-box view and the notion of a fixed self flies in the face of the psychological view of authenticity. There is an alternative.

Here is an example of how I work with my clients to increase their selves awareness and help them become more authentic at the same time. Let's look at the case of a bossy, whip-smart CFO. He was brilliant in a world of very smart people and had become the chief financial officer of a large retail organization at a very young age. At that time, the industry was beginning to experience the full business impact of Amazon and the entire Internet. In his new role, he had to help drive a new way of thinking throughout an organization of 75,000 employees as soon as possible. The technical part of his job was not a problem. Being a true business partner and helping to drive a new way of thinking throughout the organization and helping to shift the mind-set of the entire enterprise was the real challenge of his new role.

My client is straightforward, gregarious, and highly directive by nature. People would generally describe him as likeable, very smart, and bossy. He is a true extrovert who loves to take charge and direct the show. It was not working in his new higher-level role, however. How did he know this? His boss, the CEO, had told him in no uncertain terms that he was technically great but pretty much useless as a business partner trying to shift the mind-set of the entire enterprise. He reached out for help.

My first question was "are you ready to try something else?" His response was, "I am practical and I want to succeed." I took that as a yes. He needed to do something that was radically different for him. It was not going to come naturally at first. His first assignment was to listen three times more than he talked. Research and common sense tells us that listening is roughly three times as important in the art of influence as talking, so his task was to achieve a 3:1 listening-to-speaking ratio. Embodying this learning and actually interacting according to this principle is different than having an intellectual awareness. It is easy to extol the virtues of listening and much harder to actually listen more than you talk.

We devised a numerical formula for him to use as a method. He could ask clarifying questions, but he could not make a declarative statement until he had taken in three points of view. He was assigned to listen to three different people speak on any given topic before weighing in himself. You read that right: He took in three perspectives or points of view before speaking all of the time, unless it was absolutely impractical. For example, if he got a direct question from his boss like "was revenue up or down last week?" it would be impractical not to answer just as directly. In cases like that my client would answer yes or no and provide the numbers. You get the point.

At first, my CFO client struggled with the process, but over time, he began to have in-depth conversations that matter. One of those in-depth conversations was pivotal in that the director of retail operations shared that he had serious doubts about the organization's ability to keep pace in the Amazon age. After careful listening and in response to the director of retail operations' serious doubts, my client explained his point of view, which was broader as a result of his role. The director of retail operations sent him an e-mail thanking him and saying he appreciated the encouragement and sound counsel. "It seems important that our director of retail operations believes we can make the shift," my client said to me afterward. We laughed.

Was my client being authentic? Was he being genuine? Was he being fake? Which person was the real CFO? Was it the one who listened more than he talked or the one who was straightforward and directive? This story takes us to the fundamental paradox of authenticity in leadership. We think of authentic leadership as being the real us, the real deal. The problem is that there is no one real deal. There is no one single version of any of us to behold. We show different sides of ourselves in different contexts all the time. In my client's case, if he was going to succeed, he needed to bring a different side of himself to the job. His drive to succeed and make a contribution was a large part of his authentic self. His tendency to take charge and dictate was also authentic. His drive to succeed and make a contribution was a deeply held, self-concordant value. His take-charge style was habit and had worked well most of his life. He had the self-awareness to notice that his characteristic style was not working. But what happens when who we are naturally is just not effective? How do we bump up against reality, learn, and continue to become more authentic?

The larger question is how do we move from an idealistic under-standing of authenticity to a pragmatic, applied view of authenticity? Just as complex, real humans can't be reduced to just one thing, the notion of authenticity cannot be reduced to just one thing, either. As we discussed at the beginning of this chapter, psychologists have validated that the notion of authenticity consists of four interrelated processes. Authenticity is not just one thing but is multifaceted. The first and most fundamental of those facets is selves awareness.

Authentic leadership in the real world that is effective is not simply "being yourself." Being an effective, authentic leader requires being yourself with skill.[3] The reality is that you need to be your *selves* with skill. The focus of this chapter is about the first of the four research-based practices that comprise authenticity in psychological terms. The first component is selves awareness. We will cover the other three key factors in subsequent chapters. Just like my client, you are not consistent across situations. You have multiple selves and so do other people.

Self-awareness is a much-discussed concept in our culture these days and in the leadership development arena in particular. This notion of self-awareness can come across as preachy and more than a little vague. At least once every six months, I will be talking to a new client and they will look at me earnestly and say, "My boss says I need more self-awareness. Karissa, what *exactly* do I need to know about myself?" Underlying the question is a sense of confusion and a desire to understand what they need to do differently in order to be successful.

The first thing you need to understand is that situational pressures influence how we all behave. There is no fixed self you can know and then check the self-awareness box, ever. Different aspects of your selves come out in different situations. You need to work on your selves awareness, not your self-awareness. In this chapter, we will cover exactly what you need to know about your selves.

⊗⟳

ARE YOU A CHAMELEON?

Is human behavior determined by situational pressures and expectations or by personality traits? The vast majority of us tend to place more weight on personality and less on role. It always makes me laugh when a client of mine takes on a new role and finds the former person in the role exasperating. Six months into the new role, they will often say now they know why the former person acted that way. In the middle of the twentieth century, there was increased attention in the academic world on how people played roles based on expectations. In 1959 Erving Goffman wrote an influential book titled *The Presentation of Self in Everyday Life.*[4] In Goffman's view, ordinary people behaved in ways to manage the impression they were making on others. He held that much of our day-to-day social interaction was as if people were playing characters in a play. Goffman's notions are still relevant in the workplace today. If you are the leader of a team, you will behave differently than if you are the newest member of a team and are trying to figure out your place. Both the leader and the newcomer are likely to be highly attuned and managing their impressions on others to some degree.

The pendulum on this issue has swung back and forth through the years. As you might guess, there is no end to this debate of whether personality or situations determine behavior. However, psychologist Mark Snyder[5] came up with a penetrating insight that rocked the ongoing debate.

Have you ever worked with someone who seemed to be able to adjust his or her behavior in dramatic ways based on situations? I often interview people who work with my clients as part of a 360 developmental interview program and look for key overlapping themes that come up in the conversations. As a result I can tell the client exactly what is working well and exactly what they need to work on. I was interviewing people who worked for one of my clients named Barb to get some developmental feedback for her. She had recently assumed a complicated role that required her to influence people all across the globe. Fourteen people across the globe were interviewed and asked what it was like to work with Barb. As we were reviewing her findings, we discussed the fact that the Americans perceived her to be intense and collaborative, the Europeans perceived her to be relaxed and inspirational, and the team in Asia perceived her to be clear and directive. Barb had highly developed skills in adjusting and adapting her personal style to very diverse situations and audiences. Are you able to adjust your behavior in dramatic ways based on different circumstances?

Chameleons are lizards that can change colors to avoid being eaten. Much like chameleons, some people are able to change their behaviors to fit into varying situations. All of us do change our behavior to a certain degree. For example, most of us adapt and avoid talking during a prayer. However, this adjusting and adapting comes much easier to some of us than others. Social psychologist Mark Snyder referred to those who change their behavior to adapt to the situation almost effortlessly as people who are high in a psychological trait called *self-monitoring*.

People who are much more consistent across situations despite pressures to the contrary are low in self-monitoring. People who are low in self-monitoring tend to pay attention to their internal cues such as motivations, desired outcomes, and the way they are feeling that day when they are deciding how to behave. In contrast, people high in self-monitoring tend to pay more attention to external cues and demands as they are deciding how to behave. If everyone is talking quietly and beating around the bush, those high in self-monitoring tend to speak more quietly and beat around the bush. Those low in self-monitoring just may blurt out the truth in their normal tone in that situation.

Of course, leaders pay attention to both internal and external cues, but we are talking about a matter of degree here. Those who are high in self-monitoring tend to err on the side of paying more attention to the situation. Those who are low in self-monitoring tend to err on the side of paying more attention to their own internal expectations and motivations.

I always know one of my clients is low in self-monitoring when they look puzzled when I use the term *selves awareness*. They will often look disturbed and say something like, "Do you mean like multiple personalities?" I quickly say no and ask them if they can think of someone who shifts their style in dramatic ways based on different business situations. For example, could they think of a really nice guy personally who is a mean, nasty negotiator in an adversarial situation? They say yes and begin to get a sense of the idea of multiple selves. When I talk to a person who is high in self-monitoring, they really resonate with this idea that they have multiple selves. People high in self-monitoring will often say that sometimes people who are close to them have been confused by the dramatic shifts.

So, back to authenticity. Is the person high in self-monitoring less authentic? It is easy for a person who is low in self-monitoring to think so. However, whether one tends to pay more attention to internal or external cues to determine their behavior is a stable characteristic. You will have the opportunity at the end of the chapter to take the questionnaire and determine whether you are high or low in self-monitoring.

Thus, being authentic or not is more complicated and deeper than whether or not you tend to self-monitor. Think of it this way: A chameleon is not able to change its fundamental organs or nature by changing its colors. It is still a reptile trying to survive and be successful. Its changing of colors is merely an adaptation to circumstance. However, it is important for you to understand to what degree you pay attention to internal cues vs. external cues in determining how to behave as a leader in your quest to become more authentic.

Let's get practical for a moment and go back to my bossy CFO client. I did not test him for the trait of self-monitoring, but I had known both him and his boss for a while. Trust me, the CFO was low in self-monitoring and the CEO was high in self-monitoring. I had seen this CEO morph across organizations and roles and adapt in dramatic ways that seemed almost effortless to be successful across many challenging business situations. In private conversations, people who had seen the CEO across all those situations would often say they were not sure what was real and what was fake. However, the CEO's ability to self-monitor and morph was an authentic part of him. He had been that way his entire life. He grew up in a military family and had moved every two years; as a result, he had become skillful at reading situational cues and figuring out how to fit in, as a young boy. He had used those skills to his advantage in various leadership capacities.

In contrast, the CFO had been successful by being consistent across various situations. However, he was not being successful in helping shift the mind-set of the company by using his consistent characteristic style of being bossy and listening to his internal cues more than the external or situational cues. Both low self-monitoring and an intense drive to be a true business partner were an authentic part of the bossy CFO. Was the CFO being fake as he was listening three times more than he was talking, or was he being an individual capable of self-determination and bringing to life the idea of self-invention? That brings us to a discussion of free vs. fixed traits and the important work of the self-described passionate introvert Brian Little.[6]

⨋

FIXED TRAITS, FREE TRAITS, AND REAL PEOPLE

When businesspeople talk about self-awareness, they are usually referring in some fashion to what we psychologists refer to as traits. Know what your traits are and you will be self-aware, so it goes.

Not so fast. Knowing what your traits are is just the beginning of selves awareness. Henry Murray and Clyde Kluckhohn wrote a book in 1953 titled *Personality in Nature, Society, and Culture.* In that book, Kluckhorn and Murray famously said, "Every person is like all other persons, like some other people, and like no other person." Selves awareness requires you to know how you are like all other persons, like some other people, and like no other person. Your unique constellation of traits, motives, and values is rooted both in your biology and your unique history. Other people may share some of your traits, and you will experience that similarity. For example, introverts usually recognize and understand each other. When one introvert groans to another introvert that they are required to go to a big party, the other introvert understands the groan. Alternatively, extroverts also recognize themselves when they see others demonstrating classic extroverted behaviors such as being excited about a huge party with lots of new people to meet. On a macro level, we are all alike in that we are ultimately facing death and other existential issues. However, when it comes to you and what you truly value and want to express in the world, you are not just like anyone else. Who you are at a deeper motivational and values level is the result of the alchemy of your experiences and your biology.

Traits are stable, enduring aspects of your personality like extroversion and introversion, being shy or outgoing, or tending to take charge vs. hanging back and following the direction of others. The basic idea is that you need to be aware of your own personality traits and the traits of others, which will help you work more effectively with a wider variety of people.

There are many options in terms of assessment instruments designed to help people get a sense of their basic traits. Chances are you've taken the DISC, the MBTI, or one of literally hundreds of other questionnaires in the marketplace. To be sure, having a sense of your basic traits as well as the basic traits of others is useful. As you sort through all of those options in the marketplace, be cognizant that the trait dimensions that hold up the best under rigorous scientific examination are the Big Five Personality Dimensions: openness, extroversion, conscientiousness, agreeableness, and neuroticism. High scorers on openness tend to be creative, imaginative, and eccentric, and low scorers tend to be more practical and conventional. Those high in extroversion tend to be more outgoing and enthusiastic by nature. Those high in conscientiousness tend to be organized and self-directed, whereas low scorers tend to be more spontaneous. Do not be frightened by the term *neuroticism*. It just means prone to stress and worry. We are all neurotic to some degree. Agreeableness is pretty much like it sounds, meaning that if you are high in agreeableness, you are generally trusting and find it easy to get along with most people.[7] As opposed to being either one or the other of the big five, it is all a matter of degree. Moderate scores on each of the scales result in different behaviors than high or low scores. Also, a person who is high extroversion and low in agreeableness will present very differently than someone who is high extroversion and high in agreeableness.

Traits are only the beginning of selves awareness, which brings us to the work of the renowned personality psychologist Brian Little. There are three ways of being natural, according to Little. These are consistent with the bigger, broader concept of authenticity as self-invention, creation, and expression that is the thesis of this book.

The first way of being natural is to behave according to traits, or your predispositions. Back to the bossy CFO. Your natural tendency is to take charge and prescribe what everyone needs to do to make a dramatic organizational shift. So you "just do it," as Nike says.

The second way of being natural is to adapt to the culture and social norms. If the culture tends to make decisions in a participative manner, then it is possible for people to adapt and become more participative. Real people vary in their ability to adapt to cultures, though. I have worked with more than one executive who was remarkably successful in one organizational culture and crashed and burned in another one within the exact same industry. But there are certain ways in which we can all change and adapt that are unique to us. Dan P. McAdams[8] of Northwestern University uses the term *characteristic adaptations* for the ways in which we have learned to adapt that we use over and over. For example, I am not very pragmatic by nature. I love ideas and can sit around, cogitate, and imagine for hours on end happily. In big-five terms, I am extremely high on openness. However, I work with executives day in and day out who are extremely pragmatic. Early on in my career, when I was getting used to the business world, I adapted by learning to think and speak in more practical terms. Therefore, I regularly speak in very practical concrete terms, like "you need to ask three questions for every declarative statement that you make." Being really practical about psychology is a characteristic adaptation for me. I am very consistent in taking that approach. It feels natural after years of practice.

The third way of being natural is to tune into the aspects of you that are like no other person. Little terms this the "idiogenic" way of being natural. As you just learned, I could never get by with such a technical term during my client sessions, so I call it the idiosyncratic way of being authentic. What exactly does the idiosyncratic way of being authentic, or being yourself, mean?

This is about determining what is distinctive about you. Motivations and values are very individual and distinctive, as they are based on the combination of our biological predispositions and unique personal histories. This level of authenticity requires knowing what you really want, what is important to you, and why.

Back to the bossy CFO, it was really important to him to be an excellent leader who was capable of impacting the mind-set of an entire enterprise. Becoming that kind of leader was so important to him that the costs of behaving outside of his comfort zone and listening more were negligible. He was exercising what Little calls a "free trait" as he was listening carefully and avoiding making declarative statements. Free traits are those that we choose because we want to achieve a goal that is really, really important to us. The choice to behave as a listener was a free choice on the CFO's part because he was pursuing his passion of leading and influencing on a broader level. This CFO was not just trying to fit into the culture and be accepted. He desired to be a leader capable of helping the organization make a shift from a deep internal place. He was motivated intrinsically, as opposed to looking for an external reward. He certainly wanted to please his boss and do well, but more important, he truly valued excellence in everything he put his mind to.

Being a person capable of igniting an entire enterprise toward a mind-set that would be successful in the marketplace was a characteristic of his ideal self, or the kind of leader he wanted to be. The ideal self is a rich concept in the history of psychology that originated with Carl Rogers. Sometimes, we walk around aimlessly, not sure of who we want to be. The bossy CFO was sure and he moved toward the vision of his ideal self.

෨෮

THE IDEAL SELF, THE CURRENT SELF, AND LOTS IN BETWEEN

Vision statements for all kinds of businesses have become common-place. You walk into the office of almost any business and you will see statements of vision and mission literally on the walls. However, the practice of creating a vision for yourself as a leader is far less common. I am not talking about goals like getting promoted or making $200,000 or being in the top quartile. I am talking about having a vision for your leadership that goes beyond that, something like the ability to see the best in people and make them think about other possible versions of themselves at the same time. That is my authentic leadership vision. One of my client's leadership visions is to create an innovative environ-ment in which people feel safe to admit mistakes and challenge the status quo. Your vision will be specific to you, encompassing your unique collection of values, motivators, and strengths.

What is more common and often passes for leadership development is to get 360 feedback, either quantitatively or qualitatively. These 360 feedback experiences are great tools to give you a sense of your current self as a leader. The term *360* means that perceptions are gathered from your superiors, peers, and subordinates about your strengths and weaknesses as a leader. Quantitative instruments are generally computer-based and ask raters to rate you on a list of specific items that fit into a data-based competency model. In contrast, interview-based qualitative assessments are conducted when a consultant interviews a list of your colleagues and asks them all the same set of questions.

It usually plays out in the following way: Executive gets a 360 review that lists several key strengths and two or three areas of opportunity. "Areas of opportunity" is the current euphemism for "what you need to get better at." The executive goes straight to what needs to be fixed and then says to me "What do we need to do to fix this?" Let's imagine that the person is perceived to be rude and impatient. Saying "okay, I'll be polite and patient then" is not enough for a vision of who you want to be as a leader. Besides that, it won't work if you have no idea why it matters to be polite or patient. Not to mention that if you truly desire to be more respectful of others and more patient and choose that as a free trait, then we have to figure out exactly how you already behave when you are being respectful and patient. I usually have a clue what that looks like, especially if I am retained by your boss.

Who you want to be as a leader and how you want to impact other people is the key question. From the perspective of authentic leadership development, fixing the problem of rudeness requires zooming out and understanding the whole person, flaws and all. My leader clients are all both awesome and flawed. To use the term popular in the Twitterverse and used by Tyra Banks, they are *flawsome*. At the risk of making them become rude and impatient with me, I respond to the "fix it" question by answering, "I don't know. Tell me more about your rudeness and impatience!" I am trying to get a sense of the current self from their point of view. It is possible that they had little awareness of their daily rudeness and it's also possible that they had heard this a million times. I have no way of knowing without a much deeper conversation than a "fix it" chat. If I get to stay in their office longer than 15 minutes, we will have shifted gears from fixing the problem of rudeness to attacking the larger question of who they want to be as a leader. I will ask them to tell me how they would like the summary of the 360 to read. In the best of all worlds, what is their vision of themselves as an ideal leader? If you skip the all-important step of crafting a vision of who you want to be as a leader, you're not using a lever for change that will work.

If we are not crystal clear about both our ideal self and our current self, we enter into a state of cognitive dissonance.[9] *Dissonance* means discomfort. We humans like the felt sense that we are who we want to be. In a state of discomfort or dissonance, we work to either change the ideal self or the current self. The leadership development task is to keep reminding yourself of your ideal self and to remain cognizant of your current self at the same time. The cop-out is to just let both drop out of your mind and go about business as usual. You will be more comfortable, but you won't be inventing or crafting yourself as a leader, either.

Authentic leadership is about inventing and developing yourself with intention while you are in the trenches of your day-to-day work. You must really practice and work on developing yourself as you are doing your work. The self-development process is not separate from your day-to-day work life but a key aspect of it. This process is not about talking about developing an aspect of yourself but really working at it as you are meeting your commitments to your boss and to your organization. Authentic leaders who have selves awareness maintain a clear view of their current self and their ideal self as a leader. It requires both discipline and focus to continually update your vision of your ideal self and your current self.

I work with my clients to create rituals or behavioral routines in which they regularly take a look at their authentic leadership vision and get some form of feedback regarding their current self. Then, we discuss behavioral experiments designed to help bridge the gap. It is a simple (but not easy) process that gets results. Believe it or not, the bossy CFO described earlier in the chapter was described several years later by his team as not being directive enough when it was his turn to be CEO!

⤬

THE WORKOUTS

- Take 20 minutes on three consecutive days and respond to the following prompt. Just keep writing without editing. If you feel like you have written everything down, just keep writing. At the end of the three days, take a look at everything you have written and look for the ideas that mean something to you. Edit the work down to between five and seven statements. You will have a vision of who you want to be as an authentic leader.

Think about yourself as a leader in the future. Imagine you are impacting the business, other people, teams, and the organization as a whole, fully making use of your talents and all of your selves. What do you imagine?

- Go to the following website: http://personality-testing.info/tests/ SMS/. You will have the opportunity to take the self-monitoring scale. Having an understanding of your level of self-monitoring is fun and useful.

- Make a list of your free traits. What are the traits you work at because they are important in achieving something meaningful to you? Have a discussion with someone else and ask them what traits they choose to work at in order to accomplish something meaningful.

6

BALANCED PROCESSING AND COLLABORATIVE DECISION MAKING

We are all trapped in our own way of thinking, trapped in our own way of relating to people. We get so used to seeing the world our way that we come to think that the world is the way we see it.
—Brian Grazer and Charles Fishman[1]

I magine President Obama and former Speaker of the House John Boehner huddled closely doing a joint news conference to bring the nation up to speed on a decision they had just made regarding how to respond to yet another ISIS video threat. Or better yet, former Secretary of State Clinton coleading a joint task force on immigration with former Texas Governor Rick Perry.

Something perhaps more shocking than those visuals actually happened in 1861 when the most extraordinary balanced processor in

American history invited Salmon P. Chase to become Secretary of the Treasury, William H. Seward to become secretary of state, and Edward Bates to become attorney general of the United States of America. Like Rick Perry, Secretary Clinton, President Obama, and Speaker Boehner, all three of them were the rivals of this extraordinary balanced processor. This balanced processor saw them as more than rivals. He saw them as bringing complementary, different, and important skills and points of view to the table. He also saw their talents as equal to and perhaps greater than his own talents. Abraham Lincoln was the extraordinary balanced processor. He not only invited his rivals who brought different approaches and ways of thinking into the mix, but he relied heavily on them as true partners.

Many examples of Lincoln's balanced processing are contained in Doris Kearns Goodwin's *Team of Rivals*.[2] As the playing field for the presidential election in 1860 was taking shape, Lincoln was the least likely to win. He was clearly an underdog, but his ability to see himself, his opponents who later became colleagues, and the situation clearly in a balanced manner served him very well. He was not blinded by his own thinking or his own point of view. By habit and instinct, he surrounded himself with people who challenged his thinking and helped him see even more clearly.

Lincoln's abilities in this area contributed to the fact that we still have a United States of America over a century down the road. I bet you are wondering what on earth balanced processing is and if we can train our politicians how to do it immediately!

⊘

WHAT IS BALANCED PROCESSING?

Balanced processing is a research term that sounds like a new part for your computer. (You may be hearing the Intel jingle in your head.) But this less-than-sexy term gets at something really important in today's collaborative business environment.

Balanced processing is a cognitive, emotional, and behavioral skill that allows you to look at yourself, others, and situations with a broad lens that does not magnify your own view or organize everyone else's views around your own. Balanced processing is not easy, but it is essential for the practice of authentic leadership.

In the foundational piece of research on authenticity by Brian Goldman and Michael Kernis,[3] it was called unbiased processing. Their theory of authenticity in psychological terms was actually developed from recurrent, timeless themes in philosophy, and unbiased processing was what they termed one of those themes. It meant unbiased processing of information about yourself. Later researchers[4] specifically exploring authentic leadership broadened the notion of unbiased processing and changed it to balanced processing.

The presence of bias in all of our thinking is well documented within the scholarly and popular literatures. A quick Wikipedia search will explain over 100 types of common biases in daily human thought and social interaction. Balanced processing is a more practical term than the notion of being unbiased because, while it is actually possible to balance our thought process, it is naive to believe we can actually learn to think in an unbiased manner. In business, we need to bring balance to our thinking about ourselves, others, and situations. Bringing your thinking and decision making into balance is possible, but not easy. We are all a bit like fish that can't see the water. Unlike fish, we can actually survive and thrive outside of the water of our own thinking.

It is all too easy to get caught in the box of your own thinking and perspective. Brian Grazer, a successful Hollywood producer (and many would say absolute mogul), provides a great example for other executives. This is the man who produced *A Beautiful Mind, Splash, Apollo 13, Parenthood,* and many other huge box-office hits. Grazer prioritizes what he calls curiosity conversations. He has several monthly conversations with people who interest him, for the sole purpose of understanding how they think, to broaden his own view. He purposefully does not overtly connect the conversations to specific movie projects. Just like someone staying in shape physically, Grazer works at keeping his own thought process balanced by the viewpoints of others.

It takes work, effort, and attention to get out of the box of your own perceptions and broaden and balance your thought process. Balanced processing is the skill of blending your thought process with the thought processes of others without a bias toward your view. Balanced processing is the opposite of self-deception. We all know people who deceive themselves every day. You probably sit next to someone who you and everyone else knows is mediocre in terms of talent but who is convinced he or she will be the next CEO of the company. Deceiving yourself can appear to be easier, at least in the short term, than dealing with the cold, hard realities about yourself, others, or situations. We all deceive ourselves on occasion. Becoming a balanced processor is the antidote to being trapped in self-deception. How on earth are you going to be authentic and real if you can't see things, yourself, and others clearly? Balanced processing is actually a necessary ingredient for good decision making in general, not just for the practice of authentic leadership. So how do you become more like Brian Grazer and Abraham Lincoln in your quest to become an authentic leader?

First think about the following questions. These items are adapted from the Authentic Leadership Questionnaire (ALQ) created and validated by Walumbwa and associates. For our purposes, answer yes or no to the questions. But let's add another step we do not usually include in such quizzes. To fight the natural processes of bias and the rising tide of self-deception, challenge yourself to provide three recent examples of behavior to back up your claim of yes or no. Be very specific as you cite the recent examples. If you answer yes to seeking the opinions of others, name the others in each of your three examples. If you answer no, think of three decisions you made without seeking any other points of view besides your own.

Do you seek the opinions of others before making up your own mind?

Do you listen to the ideas of people who disagree with you and alter your view?

Do you take the time to listen carefully to the ideas of others before making decisions?

How did you do? When I do this with my clients, they do not get a heads-up about the examples. They just answer yes or no. Then, as we discuss, I ask for the examples including the names and so on. It can feel like an inquisition or a cross-examination in a courtroom. With a little well-timed humor and positive regard for the client emanating from me, the process usually results in the client saying, "I could do this balanced processing thing a bit more." Then, they ask, "What exactly do I need to do?" (You know my clients like the word *exactly!*)

Balanced processing is not something you can get better at due to good intentions. The theory of balanced processing is one thing, and the practice is a different ball game. It takes disciplined thinking and guts. You have to perform specific actions on a consistent basis.

Over the years, I have noticed five habits or disciplines of balanced processors. The good news is that you can make a great leap in balanced processing skills just by working at one or two of the following habits.

GET IN BALANCED PROCESSING GEAR OR NOT

Not everything requires balanced processing. The most effective balanced processors know when to get in balanced processing gear and expend all the effort it takes to get multiple points of view and really process all of that information. They also know when it is just not worth the effort to go through all of that. Balanced processing is a collaborative activity, so it takes time. We do almost everything in teams or work groups today. However, it is a myth that teams are more efficient and effective than individual decision making.[5] Richard Hackman from Harvard, who devoted his professional career to understanding and helping teams be more effective, taught us that teams make operating a business more difficult in many ways and are only effective under specific conditions, including a clear structure and expert coaching from the leader or an outside source. In my work with teams, I force them to be very structured about whether an item is for discussion or for decision. Some decisions are energy drainers for a whole team and can be addressed easily by one person or a small subteam. For example, I sat in a two-hour meeting with several high-level executives discussing where to have the Christmas party a few years back. Way too much balanced processing! As you might guess, everyone had an opinion. Finally, the operations guy lost it and said "can we make a decision on the Christmas party in the next two minutes and then deal with the fact that we have lost a hundred million in business within the last quarter?"

The first discipline of balanced processors is common sense but is often overlooked by inexperienced leaders. You have to accurately identify and categorize what you are dealing with. My grandfather always quoted Mark Twain: "If all you have is a hammer, everything looks like a nail." Authentic leaders need multiple approaches to making decisions based on what exactly they are dealing with. Simply put, is it a dilemma or a problem? One of my colleagues, Jonno Hanafin,[6] taught the leadership at a large professional services firm to regularly discriminate between problems and dilemmas in a seminar. Problems must be solved. In contrast, dilemmas must be managed. Dilemmas do not have right or wrong answers. For example, "should we invest in the future or balance the budget." This is a dilemma, not a problem. I did some of the follow-up coaching and strongly encouraged my people to say out loud "this is a problem" or "this is a dilemma" as they moved through their daily grind. You could just see the body language change as they relaxed and slowed down to deal with a dilemma and thought quickly when needing to address a problem.

Dilemma gear is different from problem-solving gear. Labeling something as a dilemma or a problem cues the brain of the individual executive well. Of course, dilemmas require balanced processing, and problems may or may not be better solved through balanced processing. Some thorny issues can have aspects of both problems and dilemmas. But for the purposes of improving your balanced processing and keeping yourself and those around you sane, start discriminating between problems and dilemmas immediately. In general, when you are facing a dilemma, label it a dilemma and seek out other viewpoints, and be very careful to balance out your own thinking with a wide variety of points of view.

In contrast, problems simply require action to meet a need. You need a spot to have the Christmas party and you choose one. The light bulb goes out and you change it. Dilemmas, on the other hand, require decisions among two or more alternatives that seem mutually exclusive but are not. Let's take one of the most common strategic business dilemmas: investing in future growth vs. tightly controlling costs. You have to do both. However, investing in the future may be more important than controlling costs at different times in the evolution of the business. Controlling costs may be key if you are not profitable.

Dilemmas are never resolved. They are just always showing up in different clothes. When a dilemma shows up in your world, intentionally get in balanced processing gear and begin balancing out your view with the ideas of other smart people. Think about how complicated it often is to decide what the right balance is between investing for the future and controlling costs. Where do we cut and where do we invest? It's a good idea to get lots of people thinking and collaborating on that.

Again, for emphasis, leaders must recognize dilemmas and get in balanced processing gear. They must also recognize problems as simple problems and either make a call or delegate a call. That is not always as easy as it sounds, as the examples are not as clear-cut as the ones provided in this section. Many of my clients have historically been so good at problem solving that they instinctively address dilemmas as if they were problems to be solved. (Remember, if all you have is a hammer, everything looks like a nail.) My advice to those clients is often to slow down and get in gear to do some balanced processing. Recognizing when to get in balanced processing gear and shifting into a slower, broader, more collaborative mode is the first and most fundamental habit of balanced processors.

❧

THREE TRICKY WORDS FOR LEADERS

People often rise to leadership roles because they are really good at their function or discipline and know most of the answers. If they don't know, they can usually figure it out either on their own or with little help from others. Becoming a leader in this way creates a form of self-reliance that has to be outgrown if you are going to be effective in more complex situations.

Bob was one of my smartest clients ever. He had a doctorate from MIT in a highly specialized technical area plus an MBA from another highly prestigious university. Not to mention he also had a great personality and was good looking to boot.

Balanced processing is a huge challenge for my smartest clients like Bob. I got to know Bob in the middle of his career during his first international assignment in which he was responsible for the Europe,

Middle East, and Africa division of the company. As his boss put it to me, Bob was crashing and burning as a leader while becoming fluent in two languages by going to night school. Bob was working harder than ever, of course. Bob's boss was concerned about the business; the team in place, which was mostly local and hard to replace; and Bob on a personal level. Members of his highly skilled team were quitting one right after the other. We had three months to figure something out or Bob was out. The pressure was on. The results were not great when he took the job, but they seemed to be declining, as opposed to improving, which was also bringing the morale of the entire team to an all-time low.

The first and most pressing issue was how to keep what was left of the team. Individual interviews with team members revealed that everyone thought Bob talked a lot for someone new who did not really understand how the business worked in vastly different areas of the world. They also viewed him as needing to be the smartest guy in the room. When pressed for what this need looked like, they mentioned things like him going into detail about particular operations and naming everyone who worked there in an effort to impress them with his memory. He also seemed to want to impress them by remembering every detail about their work and personal lives. Needless to say, no one described Bob as authentic and genuine.

What do we do when our view of the world is unsettled in such a difficult manner? These moments become a true test of one's ability to grow. I did not pull any punches when I presented the unsettling findings to Bob. He was uncharacteristically very quiet as we moved through the data. I stopped, made eye contact, and held silence on purpose. I knew we were at a defining moment, and I wanted to do everything I possibly could to help Bob move through it and be more successful. I knew my chatter to fill the void would not help. He had to have the guts to speak first. Would he pontificate and intellectualize, or was he really processing what I had said?

Bob looked at me and said, "Karissa for the first time in my work life, I don't know what to do."

I took a deep breath and knew that we had a shot. Bob had uttered three important words that are very tricky and very difficult for smart leaders: *I don't know*. Saying "I don't know" at the right times is critical in being authentic and in being successful given the complexity of our era. Moving to a better place with this team required Bob to admit to them that he did not know how to turn the business around and that he wished he could start over with the team. Two big leaps of authenticity there. Bob was not comfortable with saying any of that, but he did it anyway and he really meant it. Over several months, the team did give him another chance, and together they moved the business back into positive territory. Bob learned the importance of balanced processing and is not likely to forget it.

What are you going to do if you're a leader who really doesn't know the answer or know what to do? You must rely on others and solve the problem as a team. On an emotional level, that is very scary if you have been successful by knowing the answers. You first have to admit to yourself that you don't know, and then you have to be clear with others, both verbally and nonverbally, that you don't know. Having the guts to admit to yourself and others that you don't know is the second habit of balanced processors.

❦

Hire a Brilliant Antagonist or Three

I love it when people agree with me. It feels so good. The sheer joy of feeling right is just great. It does not feel dangerous, but the reality is that too much agreement, peace, and harmony can be dangerous in today's ever-changing business environment. The dangers of group-think termed by Irving Janis[7] are ever present. Groupthink occurs when a group makes bad decisions with negative consequences because the group begins to think alike and miss or dismiss key data points. The space shuttle *Challenger* broke apart 73 seconds into its flight on national television on January 28, 1986. On board were seven Americans from NASA, one of whom was a schoolteacher named Christa McAuliffe, who would have been the first teacher in space. The disaster happened as a result of the failure of O-rings. Understanding what an O-ring does is less important than understanding that an engineer named Roger Boisjoly predicted there was a clear and present danger the shuttle could disintegrate in exactly the way it did.

The *Challenger* example provides a vivid visual image of the dangers of groupthink. Business dilemmas are less dramatic but also have negative consequences in terms of lost opportunity and revenue. I had the chance to work with renowned strategist Vijay Govindarajan during an executive-level training in London a few years back. You could have heard a pin drop in the room when Vijay asked why Kodak had not benefited from digital photography. He continued, why did AT&T not invent and capitalize on Skype? The short answer is that both Kodak and AT&T were immersed in the world as they knew it. While no one died, Kodak used to be a dominant player in the world of cameras. In a peculiar twist of business history, Skype is owned by Microsoft. Microsoft was likely buying Skype as they were missing the first wave of tablet computing! The iPad and tablet computing as a concept were not part of the world as Microsoft knew and defined it.

Fighting the forces of groupthink or just thinking within the box of your own mind or the predominant mind-set of the company requires effort and intention. You need to be on the lookout for a brilliant antagonist or three for every team. The brilliant antagonist pushes the team's thinking in different directions and is willing to oppose the predominant view with intensity.

When I meet an executive, I am always curious about the quality of his or her team. Usually, over time, I get to meet most of the individuals on the team either socially or in a team meeting. Remember, if you want to develop your skills in balanced processing, you have to surround yourself with people who are smarter than you in general or in a specific way, and you must encourage them to disagree with you. If I start picking up that one of my executive's team is too homogeneous in the way they think, my clients hear about it. With one team of engineers, the leader and I decided to have a designated antagonist team when addressing true dilemmas. The antagonist team was tasked to prepare a case against the will of the team. Here is how it worked: The team would make a decision, everyone felt great, then the leader would task three people to work together to prepare a case for another alternative. Their job was to convince the group to do something different. Initially, the team hated the process. But two major decisions were changed as a result. The experience was eye opening for the entire team. I was thrilled when the leader asked me to meet with a potential new hire. I will never forget his words; he said, "I like this guy. He is really smart, but he comes at things from a totally different direction than I do. See what you think. I will be curious to have your point of view on him." Big leap in balanced processing! The guy was smarter than my client and was his polar opposite. He also was his choice to run the team when the client was offered a bigger, better opportunity.

Surrounding yourself with people smarter than you and who think differently will not make your life easier. But decision quality is likely to improve and your perspective will expand. So take a look at the people you work with every day. Be honest. How often do people disagree with you? How do you respond when they do? Do you really listen to the other side of the argument? Think about your boss. Does he or she have people in the inner circle who push back regularly? Do people disagree? What happens when they do? A true authentic leader who is working at balanced processing will listen carefully. Based on how the leader responds when someone disagrees, they are more or less likely to disagree again. When someone has the courage to disagree with authority, the way the boss responds either creates a climate for balanced processing or not. Authentic leaders with balanced processing ability welcome the smart antagonists and, most important, their views.

⸎

Know and Own All Your Biases

Although it is impossible to think in an unbiased manner, it is important to understand common biases. We will cover two types of biases in this section that balanced processors need to understand and own about themselves. The first type of bias is more general. These typical biases affect the vast majority of humans to a greater or lesser degree. Psychologists have validated their existence over and over. The second type of bias you will discover is rooted in your personal history and unique to you. This less well-known type of bias goes back to the work of an under-appreciated psychologist of the last century named George Kelly.[8]

First let's dig into the three most common recurrent cognitive biases. The first one is *overconfidence bias*. There is a natural human tendency to overestimate our personal competence. Research psychologists ask people to complete questionnaires with actual, factual, right-or-wrong answers just like tests. Then, they ask how confident people are that they were right. When they say they are 100 percent confident they are right, they tend to be 70–80 percent correct. Overconfidence bias tends to make us think we got the right answer when we did not, or that the blow-up we just had on one of our best employees will soon be forgotten.

As previously mentioned, balanced processing has to do with how you relate to yourself, other significant people, and situations. This one primarily gets at how you think about yourself. I know my clients are really starting to get this one when they say things like, "At the risk of sounding overconfident, I think I got through to him." The quickest way to convince people of your inauthenticity is to be overconfident and overestimate your own abilities in general. Authentic leaders understand overconfidence bias and adjust their self-perceptions accordingly. Remember, overconfidence bias is found in the majority of the population, but you could be an outlier. Some of my clients through the years have had an underconfidence bias that made them work hard and be wildly successful, particularly in zero-mistake environments like nuclear power.

Anchoring bias accounts for lots of errors in decision making. Anchoring bias simply means that what we hear first sticks with us more.[9] Imagine that you are overseeing several manufacturing plants. You get a call over the weekend from a plant manager in Spokane. He says there has been an incident in the plant and three people have been hurt. The plant manager says: "One of our operators went to sleep at 2:30 AM and did not see the hazard light on the control panel for machine 48 in the back corner. Three workers came over to move the raw materials and they were badly burned because the machine had overheated."

By Monday, the details have been sorted out and an investigation has made it clear that the hazard light never came on in the control room. The plant manager is passing the information along to his boss, who is convinced of a cover-up. Boss goes ballistic. Keep in mind that this was the first safety incident in years and there is a logical explanation for why the plant manager initially thought the guy on the control panel went to sleep. But there is no convincing the boss. This is an example of anchoring bias. What you or anyone else hears first, especially in a new or ambiguous situation, carries more weight. Keep that in mind always. The most common example is the power of first impressions. It can take years and a lot of effort to overcome a bad first impression due to the power of anchoring bias.

The third and final bias that you need to watch out for is called the *availability bias*. We tend to be way too heavily influenced by information that is readily available, more recent, or creates a vivid image.[10] Think about a personal relationship with a friend or significant other. If you just had a big fight with that person and I ask "how is your relationship going?" you are more likely to say negative things. But if I ask you the next week, you will be less likely to be negative if you have not fought within the last week. As one of my clients used to say, do great things right before and during performance review season. I used to laugh because he would wait to tell his boss about some of his accomplishments until closer to performance review time.

In your quest to be a balanced processor, be aware that you will be unduly influenced by things that are top of mind unless you actively work to fight the availability bias. This one deserves special consideration, given that so much information is readily available on Google. However, there are few controls to ensure accuracy. The bottom line is just because it is easy to get information does not mean it is actually helpful, relevant, or accurate. But your mind and my mind are unduly influenced by what is close at hand and easy to obtain.

We have been delving into biases that affect all of us to some degree or another. We are all vulnerable to having our judgment clouded by availability bias, anchoring bias, or overconfidence bias. We can't stop there, though. We also have biases that are unique to us that are rooted in our personal histories. In order to be more balanced in our decision making, we need to be aware of what personality psychologist Kelly called our personal constructs. In Kelly's view, we are all actively producing theories about how we think the people and situations around us work. We use these theories to predict the behavior of others. We are all like scientists forming theories and testing them all the time. A personal construct has two extreme points like happy/sad, tech savvy/not tech savvy, introvert/extrovert, or hard worker/lazy. We all have certain personal constructs that we use regularly to make sense of ourselves, other people, and the world. The ones that are used the most are core to us and are core personal constructs.

Let me give you an example. I was asked to assess two candidates for a high-level role in a retail company. Through several discussions, three characteristics were deemed key to the new executive being successful: driving change, strategic agility, and approachability. The company was in the midst of significant change like everyone else. Strategic agility mattered because the team believed the fundamental direction of the business was likely to shift in the next few years. Finally, approachability was a core personal construct of the CEO. He did not like people who were uppity in his view. He had grown up poor and hated uppity people. Just like Kelly would have predicted, the CEO evaluated whether he wanted to be around you or not based on whether you were uppity or approachable.

The assessment process consisted of a three-hour interview, an IQ test, and a personality test. Let me tell you about the two candidates. The first candidate was MENSA smart and had an extroverted personality made for the hand-to-hand combat of the retail industry. His experience base was such that he had led two very significant strategic changes in another company. Strategic agility, check. The second candidate was bright enough but not MENSA smart. He was more reserved personality-wise and had spent several years at McKinsey doing strategy consulting. I was struck by his ideas and optimism about the existing business. Overall, he was the kind of guy who would make a great dinner companion. The time comes for me to report my assessment findings. I walk through each of the candidate's strengths and weaknesses. Both would be a good choice, but the first candidate was stronger in my view due to the depth of his actual experience in demonstrating strategic agility vs. consulting on strategic issues. I notice that my CEO client is frowning at me. We engage in active dialogue. That is code for he has hired me to be an antagonist in this situation and hopefully, I am being brilliant. This goes on for 45 minutes and we part deciding to sleep on it.

I promptly call him the next morning to continue our discussion but also to make sure that he is not going to fire me. I had pushed back pretty hard and he was a great client. We are chatting and he says:

"Karissa, I just can't see trusting a person with this level of responsibility, who came to a meeting with me in a Kmart sports jacket. If everything that you say about this candidate is true, why does he not get a better sports jacket?" Internally, I laugh and think that I should have seen this coming. I let myself off the hook because I understand fabric quality better if we are talking about womenswear.

On a more serious note, we had just uncovered another one of my client's personal constructs. Those who dress well vs. those who do not was a way he made sense of other people. Clearly, those who dressed well were more competent in general, in his view. He hired the well-dressed candidate and came to find out the well-dressed candidate struggled with the strategic-agility aspect of his job and needed coaching. I was ready to provide that coaching, and it was a win-win of sorts!

Think about the previous example. Notice the uniqueness of my client's system of personal constructs. Uppity vs. approachable was about a way of interacting with people, in his mind. You spoke to people, knew their names, and looked them in the eye if you were approachable. Being well-dressed or not had nothing to do with whether you were uppity or not. Being well-dressed or not was a separate and unrelated personal construct. All of our personal constructs and biases are unique to us. We need to know what they are and not expect them to be logical. They just are what they are.

What are some of your personal constructs that can bias your view of other people or situations? What polarities or opposites do you habitually use to categorize other people? The awareness of your personal biases is critical in becoming a more balanced processor. My client and I laughed for years about the case of the Kmart sport coat. He still surrounds himself with well-dressed and approachable people who are not uppity according to his particular definitions of uppity and well-dressed.

❦

HAVE A BIG EGO AND PUT IT ON THE SHELF

In the spirit of knowing and owning your biases, I admit that I am a Jamie Dimon fan. (In 2015, Jamie Dimon had been chairman, president, and chief executive officer of JPMorgan Chase for more than a decade). I have become a fan by watching how he handles himself as he has been hauled in front of Congress on multiple occasions in recent years. Knowing that my judgment may very well be compromised by admiration, let me tell you why I am a fan. Although I am sure he is a complex character with multiple sides, some of which can be very difficult to deal with for those who know him well, he has artfully put his ego on the shelf and maintained a strong point of view at the same time as he has dealt with Congress on multiple occasions during the last few years. That is one seriously difficult dance.

Although the cynic in you may be saying anyone could handle that with enough public relations coaching, his self-presentation in those situations in front of Congress is consistent. Given how many times he has been in front of Congress and how consistent he has been, my hypothesis is that he has the ability to put his ego on the shelf at the right time for the good of the enterprise as a whole. When in front of Congress, Jamie maintains his contrite body language, explains the issues in terms that are clear but not talking down to people, admits mistakes, and lays out corrective action every time. My favorite appearance actually goes back to 2008 during the TARP era when they asked him what they should do if he came back needing money again and he said, "If that happens, it won't be me coming back!"

It takes a strong ego and a strong point of view to lead in complex organizations. The word *ego* has unfairly gotten a bad reputation. Ego simply means a sense of yourself. Putting that ego on the shelf at the right time can make a difference in business terms but also in the process of becoming more authentic. Having a big ego and putting it on the shelf at the right time is the last discipline in this chapter, for good reason. It is the most difficult of the practices and it may very well play a role in all of the others. You have to put your ego on the shelf to say "I don't know." You have to challenge your own point of view (the water you swim in) in order admit your biases. Working every day with people as smart as you who are going to challenge you does not always make you feel good. It takes a lot of confidence or what I call a big ego to tolerate constant pushback on what you think.

THE WORKOUTS

- Go have coffee with someone who has diametrically opposed political views. Go right for the hot-button questions and ask them who they are supporting for president and why. Ask them questions and attempt to understand why they believe what they do. It is more fun if you pick someone that you like. Do not argue.

- Analyze your current job. How much of what you deal with in an average day are problems that must be solved vs. ongoing dilemmas? Are you collaborating enough on the dilemmas? Are you pulling the trigger and executing with just a few people on simple problems when appropriate? We are in an era in which it can be the default to try to put a team on everything. It may or may not be a good idea.

- For a week, write down every time you say "I don't know." You have to say "I don't know" out loud for it to count. Simply thinking it is not enough to hit the log. For some of us, that is hard. During the next week, write down every time you say "I'm wrong" out loud and in public. That is hard for others of us. Learning how to verbalize both phrases is essential in becoming a balanced processor. If you never use either phrase, you know where you need to start.

7

RELATIONAL TRANSPARENCY AND HONEST CONVERSATIONS

You can't manage a secret.
——Alan Mulally, former CEO, Ford Motor Company[1]

While I have never denied my sexuality, I haven't publicly acknowledged it either, until now. So let me be clear: I'm proud to be gay, and I consider being gay among the greatest gifts God has given me. Being gay has given me a deeper understanding of what it means to be in the minority and provided a window into the challenges that people in other minority groups deal with every day. It's made me more empathetic, which has led to a richer life. It's been tough and uncomfortable at times, but it has given me the confidence to be myself, to follow my own path, and to rise above adversity and bigotry. It's also given me the skin of a rhinoceros, which often comes in handy when you are the CEO of Apple.
——Tim Cook, Apple CEO, to *Bloomberg Business*[2]

My client's eyes were tearing up as she declared, "I feel shell-shocked." Barb had been recently promoted to the role of chief information officer in a division of a large financial services organization. Barb had progressed up the ladder through the years in the male-dominated world of financial services and information technology by working hard and inspiring loyalty from anyone and everyone who had ever worked for her. She never asked anyone to do anything she would not do herself. Barb was a Midwestern farm girl with a value system that held respect for everyone, and they felt it.

For the first time in her career, she was struggling in her new role. She also had a new boss who demanded that the information technology function be a strong business partner with clear opinions, ideas, and pushback on the lines of business when needed. I was serving as Barb's coach and advisor with the explicit goal of helping her be successful in the new role. We had drafted a focused plan for her executive development and had just reviewed the plan with Barb's boss, the president of the division.

As we were concluding the meeting, Barb's boss looked her straight in the eye and said: "You have to stop acting like you are glad to be here. You are too eager. You belong here. You will get over being glad to be at the table. Then, you will be more effective."

We sat there in silence for a few moments as the raw honesty of the boss's words hit with a thud. I had been in similar meetings with this boss before. That raw honesty was part of her brand, and for some people it was just too much. Such people could not cut it on her team. This was Barb's first experience with such raw honesty in a 27-year corporate career. Hence, the shell-shocked feeling.

As Barb and I meandered back to her office, she gathered her composure and said, deadpan, "That was an honest conversation." We laughed out loud. Barb had related the obvious: that it would have been easier and much more comfortable for everyone if her boss had avoided being that honest. Barb continued by saying, "I think I will ultimately appreciate it." And she did ultimately appreciate it. Within the next year, Barb had moved to the next level of success. Her confidence also soared. Cheers to the power of an honest conversation with your boss! Before we celebrate and simplify too much, let's ask a great, but rather obvious question.

At the time this meeting took place, Barb had enjoyed a successful 27-year career in three different top-drawer corporations. Why on earth had she never had such an honest conversation before? But Barb is not alone.

⚬⚬⚬

THE VALUE OF HONEST CONVERSATION

When was the last time you had a conversation at work that was that honest with your boss? Or with a peer or a subordinate? It has become fashionable to use the term "transparency," and "transparent leadership" is viewed as a positive thing in theory. But the leadership practice of transparency, which creates honest, substantive conversations, is far from routine in most work environments. Holding back and taking a stance of "you first" on this transparency thing is an all-too-easy choice.

Authentic leaders are willing to go first and demonstrate transparency and openness. I am not talking about the kind of brutal honesty when you get mad and fire off a nasty-gram via e-mail. I am talking about an honest conversation in which you searched inside yourself and expressed what you really thought about something. Your words were not empty or superficial or in corporate speak, but were carefully chosen and deeply felt. When was the last time you had a thoughtful, intentional, honest conversation that you knew involved personal risk and chose to have the conversation anyway?

Our exploration in this chapter is about relational transparency and the importance of honest conversations in becoming an authentic leader and your best self. Relational transparency is one dimension of psychological authenticity. It is not all there is to authentic leadership, but you cannot be an authentic leader without having the courage to be transparent and have honest conversations at the right times. Transparency isn't simple or straightforward or easy, but transparency matters a lot. There are many reasons to avoid being transparent at work, including the risk of being rejected by others, the reality that the messenger delivering bad news about the business could be shot, and the fact that it takes a lot of work to intentionally and thoughtfully tell the truth.

This brand of transparency is also not about spouting off whatever is on the top of your mind and heart. Spouting off—virtually or in person—is simply an expression of immaturity. The transparency of authentic leadership that is a force for both generating positive business results and making the world a better place is demonstrated in the epigraphs that start this chapter.

TRANSPARENCY THAT CREATES BUSINESS RESULTS

Let's start with the first epigraph from Alan Mulally, who led the remarkable transformation of Ford Motor Company from the brink of disaster between 2006 and 2014. The full story of the turnaround is documented in journalist Bryce G. Hoffman's excellent book *American Icon: Alan Mulally and the Fight to Save Ford Motor Company*. Hoffman conducted extensive interviews with Mulally and other key Ford executives as he penned the remarkable story.

During those interviews, Mulally said to Hoffman, "You can't manage a secret." In other words, problems cannot be solved without the information on the table. Ford Motor Company was obviously full of problems in 2006, given that the company had lost $6 billion in the third quarter alone. What seemed obvious to an outsider or anyone owning the stock was not so obvious (and was certainly not being addressed) inside the company. When Mulally arrived in 2006, he uncovered one secret after another and an absolute lack of honest conversations about what was really happening at Ford. Mulally came into the auto industry as an outsider after a storied career at Boeing. He brought a positive attitude and an absolute commitment to transparency. He instituted weekly business plan review meetings with his executive team early on in his tenure. During these meetings each member of the executive team was required to provide an update on their progress toward the plan each week. Not only were they to provide an update, they were to color code their results as red, green, or yellow. Green meant good progress toward the plan in that executive's area of accountability. Red meant that there was trouble in their function or line of business or major project. Yellow meant danger and was used to signal caution and concern. Team members strongly resisted the idea of even appearing at these meetings, but Mulally persisted and forced attendance.

For weeks, every member of the team presented nothing but green lights, meaning that everything was just great and going just fine in his or her individual area of the business. Meanwhile, the enterprise continued to bleed money. The existing culture of the company and the executive team was to protect yourself at all costs. Admitting to problems was perceived as a sure way to get fired.

In stark contrast, Mulally envisioned and embodied a different, more transparent approach, in which executives came into the room and threw tough issues on the table and helped each other solve real problems. But the existing culture was so internally combative and competitive that the head of the North American automotive business, Mark Fields, who had been a rising star in the company prior to the hiring of Mulally, assumed that Mulally would fire him eventually. So Fields decided to go out with a bang and admit to several key issues in the North American business by throwing up yellow and red lights during the weekly meeting.

To the shock of the team, Mulally literally clapped his hands when Fields's presentation ended. Despite the clapping, everyone in the room still assumed that Fields would not be at the next meeting, as he was sure to be fired. However, Fields was at the next meeting and the next. Mark Fields had started a trend. Other members of the team started admitting problems by throwing up red and yellow lights. After the team members started being transparent with each other, Mulally knew it was possible to save the American icon of Ford Motor Company. (Incidentally, Mark Fields succeeded Mulally as CEO in 2014. As of today's date, he still has not been fired.)

It is a part of human nature to be self-protective, and it takes intention and commitment to overcome those all-too-human internal barriers. The story of Ford Motor Company teaches that the power of transparency can transform a business—even when it's pretty far gone. Authentic leaders have the courage to go first and actively work to overcome barriers such as those experienced by Ford by laying out expectations for transparency and then setting the example of dealing with actual issues. It is critical that leaders communicate to their people that problems can exist in a business without the person being the problem. That is easier said than done. But transparency is fast becoming a necessary way of leading in this complicated, fast-changing business landscape of the twenty-first century. The honest conversations are not just the right thing to do. Operating with enough transparency to deal with the issues quickly could very well be key to staying relevant in your market space. Leaders have no choice but to step up and demonstrate the willingness to deal with the good, the bad, and the ugly in regard to the business dynamics in this era. In order to succeed, leaders must create cultures in which there is transparency regarding the business dynamics. It is possible to make transparency a norm in an organization or a team, but as the story of Alan Mulally and the transformation of Ford Motor Company shows, it isn't easy.

⸎

EMOTIONAL TRANSPARENCY MATTERS, TOO

The second epigraph is a demonstration of transparency that is not directly related to a business issue. When Tim Cook came out as a gay man in *Bloomberg Business* in October of 2014, he demonstrated a level of emotional transparency that would not have been expected or welcomed in the twentieth century. In the epigraph Cook talks about his personal struggle and the fact that he has never lied nor has he ever been really open about his sexual orientation before, either. This kind of emotional transparency is different from the transparency about what is really going on in the business. How important is this type of emotional transparency that technically has nothing to do with the business? Is it important? Does it matter? Norms are changing quickly regarding the expectations of emotional transparency for leaders.

While on vacation, Facebook COO Sheryl Sandberg's husband died unexpectedly of a heart attack. Sandberg could have chosen to be silent and guarded as she worked through her own grief, but she made the choice to be brutally honest about the raw pain of the shocking loss in a recent Facebook post. She describes going to a parent-child event at the children's school in the post. Sandberg writes, "So many of the parents—all of whom have been so kind—tried to make eye contact or say something they thought would be comforting. I looked down the entire time so no one could catch my eye, for fear of breaking down." If you have ever experienced intense grief, you have lived the exact moment she describes where you are reengaging with your life, but terrified of breaking down emotionally at any minute. With her words, we feel that despite her extraordinary accomplishments, she is human and someone that we can all relate to. In the twenty-first century, we are looking for leaders who are extraordinary but relatable. The relatable aspect comes in large part from the choices leaders make around emotional transparency. The key word in regard to emotional transparency is *choice*. How much is appropriate? How much is too much? What purpose does this kind of emotional transparency serve?

In the spirit of transparency, I must say that I don't have all the answers on this one. Individual leaders struggle mightily with emotional transparency in regard to heartbreak, illness, and shortcomings, just to name a few of the typical struggles. Sandberg and Cook provide two dramatically different examples. Even the venues selected point out the fact that Tim Cook and Sheryl Sandberg are wired very differently. Cook chose *Bloomberg Business*, a prestigious business outlet, and Sandberg chose Facebook, which is much more accessible. Cook's statement is also much more distant vs. emotionally raw and immediate. Cook had made peace with his sexual identity years ago. In contrast, Sandberg was still in the midst of an emotional struggle to accept the death of her husband.

Individual leaders must figure out how to navigate the big emotional transparency questions for themselves in a way that is true to who they are. In advising leaders, what's right for one isn't right for another. The key question is, "What's right for you?"

That being said, I do often ask my clients to challenge themselves. People tend to fall into the category of being too transparent or too opaque about their emotions. I think of the more opaque ones as cautious souls and the more emotionally transparent ones as open books. I often ask the more opaque, distant ones to do something such as talk about a personal weakness in a meeting. They look terrified at the very idea. But more times than not, the more emotionally cautious ones learn it is safe to be more transparent, and other members of the team are impacted positively by their disclosure.

Now, I'm not asking these cautious souls to do anything dramatic. They are just being 5 percent more transparent than before. On the flip side, I often ask my clients who are more open-book types to refrain from disclosing their frustration or some other intense emotion for 24 hours. That too creates interesting learning. Let me give you an example. One of my open-book types was intensely frustrated with a project team and wanted to let them have it. I asked him to refrain from expressing his emotions for 24 hours. As he said, it was telling that he didn't feel as frustrated by the next day. (It would also have been telling had he been more frustrated.) My client commented that while he still felt frustrated the next day, he also recognized that the team was facing an obstacle that no one—including himself—saw coming. When he addressed the team, he talked about how frustrating it is to deal with unexpected issues. He went on to tell a story of a time when he led a project team that dealt with several unforeseen obstacles successfully and how they went on to accomplish the goal anyway. The team was energized and served by his broader perspective. He needed those 24 hours to broaden his perspective, though.

Despite my categories, none of us are truly open books or cautious souls. Transparency of all kinds—including emotional, cognitive, behavioral, or the business and organizational kind—is *not* an all-or-nothing proposition in the real world. The notion of total transparency is a myth that must be debunked in order to get down to the business of getting better at the transparency dimension of authentic leadership.

⬥⬥⬥

THE MYTH OF TOTAL TRANSPARENCY

Most of us tend to think of transparency as an "either/or" thing. Someone is not transparent and that is a bad thing. We usually mean they are hiding something from us. Another person is transparent and that is a good thing. We feel like they are being open and transparent with us. But if we really think about this issue of transparency at a deeper level, the plot thickens. How many of us are completely transparent with ourselves at all times? Are you sure you even know exactly what you are feeling and thinking at any given moment? Stop a moment and take that thought in.

If we can't even be sure of everything that is going on in our own heads and hearts, how can we assume someone else is being totally transparent? So, the first rule of the territory is that there is no such thing as total psychological transparency. That is what I call the myth of total transparency. Transparency at work is always a matter of degree, intention, choice, relevance, and appropriateness.

The Pixar animated feature *Inside Out* [3] takes us inside the mind of 11-year-old Riley as she experiences the trauma of a move to a new school in a new state and the movie provides a vivid illustration of why there is no such thing as total transparency. *Inside Out* begins at a relatively simple control panel located in Riley's mind, which manages the vast territory of her 11-year-old brain with the emotion of joy dressed in a spiffy outfit at the helm. The control panel is simple enough to comprehend quickly with just a few knobs, gears, and options. As the movie progresses, it becomes clear that the experience of moving to a new school has challenged Riley's brain. Through the process of dealing with the challenge and learning, Riley's brain has become more complex. Hence, the control panel looks quite daunting toward the end of the movie, with many more options on the control panel alongside new gears, knobs, and monitors. And there is a new gear called puberty! As we all know, puberty makes everything even more complicated.

My point here is that because there is so much going on in the mind and heart of any of us at any given time, there is no way we can be totally transparent. Transparency is always a matter of degree. Authentic leaders, however, are at the control panel of their own minds and hearts. That is easier said than done. The pace of leading in a large organization is fast and intense. Taking the time to ground yourself enough to stay in touch with your own control panel requires discipline. I require most of my clients to mandate time to think on their calendars. If they don't maintain that discipline, it is easy to spin out of control and have no idea what is going on in the vast territory of your own mind and heart.

While there is no such thing as total transparency, the issue of transparency is at the forefront of expectations for leaders in the twenty-first century. As you will discover in the next section, the world has changed and is changing at a rapid pace toward more openness, and it is becoming much harder to keep a secret.

THE AGE OF TRANSPARENCY

Unless you have been living under a rock, you are aware that the twenty-first century is all about access, openness, and transparency. There is always a new app designed to help you share your life, thoughts, or general information in a new way. For all of the positive qualities and possibilities, this age of transparency poses some tough challenges for all of us. Who among us has not sent an e-mail that was instantly regretted? Or had a friend post a photo of us on Facebook that made us cringe? It is difficult to hide anything. There is a record somewhere of all of your e-mails, and all kinds of famous people have been videotaped doing terrible things.

All of this access and transparency is especially hard for large organizations and their leaders. Consider the following quote from Don Tapscott, the author of *The Naked Corporation: How the Age of Transparency Will Revolutionize Business*:[4] "The term 'open' is rich with meaning and positive connotations. Amongst other things, it is associated with candor, freedom, flexibility, expansiveness, engagement, sharing, and access. However, it is not an adjective that has traditionally been used to describe organizations. Words like *insular, bureaucratic, hierarchical, secretive,* and *closed* often apply much better."

If you believe we do what works, it is hard to deny that the insular and closed way of running organizations worked well throughout most of the twentieth century. In the United States in particular, we enjoyed a great boom of economic growth in the post–World War II era, heralded largely by the triumphs of large organizations that were insular and closed but provided stable employment to millions of people.

Zoom to our current era. Think about the U.S. government's struggle with WikiLeaks and Edward Snowden—those were just a couple of transparency dramas that we all got to witness on television. Relationships between the United States and key allies, especially Germany, were damaged by the disclosure that the United States government had been monitoring the cell phone calls of German Chancellor Angela Merkel.

Large organizations, including sovereign governments and large corporate entities in particular, have historically been anything but transparent. The lack of external transparency has historically been mirrored inside big organizations as well. General business information and/or personal performance information has been anything but transparent within large bureaucratic organizations. Hence, someone like Barb could have a very successful career without ever having to deal with an honest conversation like the one she had with her boss. Old habits die hard, and the vast majority of C-level leaders are attempting to adjust to this new era of transparency both internally and externally.

Traditionally, the general rule of the game was to err on the side of secrecy. But as Warren Bennis and James O'Toole effectively argue in their 2009 *Harvard Business Review* article "A Culture of Candor,"[5] the rules of the game have changed dramatically. Bennis and O'Toole argue that in this era, leaders would do well to err on the side of transparency when in doubt. By that they mean err on the side of transparency in general and with everyone, including customers, suppliers, employees, and all stakeholders. Hence, their view of transparency is much broader than just financial.

So what's a leader to do? The ability to be transparent, have honest conversations, and build real relationships comprises one of the four key elements of authenticity in psychological terms. To be sure, there are valid reasons for the historical secrecy and control of information at the institutional level. However, it is a new day. Everyone has access to information, and leaders need to model openness and transparency—it is critical in order to motivate followers toward a higher level of openness and collaboration. Getting things done requires coordination and openness, often across continents. Moving at the speed of business today requires interpersonal transparency, cooperation, and collaboration. To be sure, there are still organizations that are functioning according to the twentieth-century model and struggling mightily with this new day. At the organizational level we are in a period of transition. In my day-to-day consulting, I see facets of the old way and other behaviors that are representative of the new way in the same organization—all on the same day. However, it's clear that organizational norms are moving in the direction of transparency.

As previously mentioned, there are also risks for individual leaders in being *too* transparent. Authentic leaders must understand the risks of personal transparency. Do we really want to know the dirty laundry of the leaders we respect or would like to respect? Where are the lines? On the other hand, people want to be led by other people they can understand. People need to relate to their leaders in genuine, real ways. Where is the balance? What works? People overwhelmingly say they want leaders who are transparent and real. You have probably said it yourself. But if you are honest, you struggle at times with how transparent to be. We all do. We do not want to risk being rejected.

What can leaders do to model the way of appropriate transparency and create cultures in which information flows and the right things get done? In working with leaders, I offer three general rules that are helpful in navigating this complicated transparency terrain. We will delve into each of the three general rules in the following section.

⸙

GENERAL PRACTICAL RULES OF THE TRANSPARENCY ROAD

The first general rule is to practice proactive transparency. Most leaders think of transparency as being related to a specific issue: "Should I tell the truth about the fact that we are laying people off?" "Should I let people know I am getting a divorce?"

I redirect my leaders to think about transparency in a broader way. How do you make sure over time that people feel like they know who you are as a leader and a human being? That is the key question. What are you doing on a daily basis to help people understand who you are and where you are coming from? Behaving on a daily basis in ways that help people understand who you really are is the practice of proactive transparency. You have to think about it, but it is not hard. Practically speaking, if people feel like they have a general sense of who you are—or, put another way, like they "get" you—whether or not you are transparent regarding single issues becomes much less important. (That is true unless the single issue is something blatantly unethical.) But if the single issue is that you don't tell people you are getting a divorce or that a layoff is coming, those are gray issues in the view of most people. In practicing proactive transparency, you give people a broader view and a window into who you are regularly. They have a lot more context to draw from in understanding who you are as a leader and what you are about.

How exactly does one practice proactive transparency? The primary tool of proactive transparency is telling your stories in an intentional, thoughtful way. True stories about your early life and the key experiences that shaped who you are as a person are especially potent. It is important that the stories be real in that you don't present fairy tales but give people a sense of your struggles and how you navigated through significant challenges.

Let me offer you an example of a business leader and friend who artfully used the story about how he became so successful and taught us all that transparency was a force in human relationships no less powerful than the sun. This is the story of Matt Haley, who embodied proactive transparency and being comfortable with your origins in life as a business leader. Matt was the 2014 recipient of the James Beard Humanitarian of the Year award and the founder of a restaurant empire consisting of nine successful restaurants, gross sales of $80 million, and an engaged workforce in a transient and tough industry. The James Beard Awards are like the Oscars of the restaurant industry.

What kind of person are you imagining as I describe Matt's business accomplishments and the fact that he won the Humanitarian of the Year award from the prestigious James Beard Foundation? What does the person you are imagining look like? What is his background?

The real Matt was a recovering addict, ex-convict, and an abuse victim, who grew up in a violent home where his father beat his mother. As opposed to quietly processing all of this in a therapy room and keeping his successful businessman persona separate, Matt told his stories of prison and the rough times of his childhood at every opportunity. He connected the dots between his rise from prison to dishwasher to successful entrepreneur to the power of hard work and the fact that everyone deserves a second chance. He often said the restaurant industry had given him a shot and he was going to give others a shot. Now that theme will engage your workforce. People in Matt's company are not just putting out crab cakes. They are demonstrating that they can deliver something of value in the community. He connected his story with the business demands in a way that was truly authentic in the best sense of the word.

Matt died in a motorcycle accident in 2014 while in India. In one of our last conversations, he had the audacity to say to me, "Doc, you need to tell your story." How dare he tell me, someone whose expertise and experience is in getting others to open up, to open up! He challenged me to be more transparent, and my life is all the richer as a result of his example and prompting.

So find ways to tell your stories. No one else can do it. Make thinking about and telling your stories a focus in your leadership development. Start where you are comfortable and build out from there. Bill George[6] advocates focusing specifically on your crucibles or the difficult experiences in both your business and personal life that made you who you are. The task is to allow people to see the struggle and how you found your way to the other side of tough and difficult challenges.

The second general rule for navigating the transparency road as a leader is to mind the gap between your persona and reality. The word *persona* means playing your social role as you are supposed to. The original Latin word from which persona is derived literally means "theatrical mask." As Erving Goffman points out in his classic sociological treatise *The Presentation of Self in Everyday Life*,[7] this notion of persona or social role in everyday life is relatively new in terms of human history. Playing roles was often thought of as part of theater for the majority of human history. In the agrarian age where everyone was trying to survive on a farm, people did not think about their image. Neither did the cavemen and women. Modernization in the twentieth and twenty-first centuries has certainly upped the ante on playing your role or having a persona.

It's naive to believe that you don't need to have a persona. For example, my professional persona is of a person who tends to dress quite fashionably, formally, and appropriate for a boardroom. (At least that is how I hope I am perceived!) Right now, I am sitting here writing in jeans and flip-flops. If I showed up at a client site in this current get-up, they might look for a psychologist for me. Crafting a professional persona is adaptive and necessary in our current visual world. However, we need to mind the gap between our deepest, most real selves and our persona. "Mind the gap" is what they say in the UK subway system so that you won't fall between the train car and the platform and get hurt. The idea is to pay attention to the gaps between your persona and the real you. There *will* be gaps; that is just reality. But you do not want them to grow too large. You and others can get hurt. We all know stories of moral crusader types who have dark secrets that come out where we learn that they are engaging in the behavior they are crusading about. That's an extreme example, but you get the point.

Craft your persona carefully from the inside out with awareness of your audience, but do not let your audience dictate your persona. Let your persona be crafted based on interaction between who you really are and the demands of your circumstances. Take me and the snappy dresser thing. Despite my current state of dress, there is a part of me that really loves great fabric and nice clothing. It is not fake, but it is a persona.

The third general rule is a watch-out. Avoid empty words and double-talk. It is better to say less if you can't say anything substantive or of value. People in positions of authority tend to prattle when they are anxious or trying to avoid saying something they know people will not like. In this age of too much information, people's radar for prattle is escalating, and they will tune you out or lose trust in you.

Lucy Kellaway is an English columnist and has written on workplace issues in the *Financial Times* for several years. In July 2015 Lucy's column was titled "Microsoft Mission Statement: So Many Words, Most of Them Empty."[8] Lucy had been forwarded a 1,500-word e-mail the CEO of Microsoft, Satya Nadella, had circulated to all employees. In the column Lucy walks through the e-mail describing the blend of what she termed "mishmash," euphemisms, and corporate speak. The new Microsoft mission, "to empower every person and every organization on the planet to achieve more," was unveiled in the e-mail with the appropriate digital drumroll. To be sure, Lucy tends to be critical of senior leaders in the United States; however, her questioning what exactly that mission statement language means does resonate. Buried deep within the very grandiose upbeat e-mail was the term "tough choices." Everyone knows "tough choices" is code for layoffs. This is not an easy message to deliver, and I am not advocating that the e-mail should have just announced the naked truth without any context. The broader context is relevant. But leaders need to keep in mind that the prattle meter is ticking. It is best to avoid empty words as much as possible.

❧❦❧

THE CHALLENGE OF TRANSPARENCY

There is nothing more challenging for leaders than navigating the terrain of relational transparency. Transparency and honesty have the potency of the sun. The sun lights up the world and makes things grow, but too much of it can do a lot of damage. As you have learned, total transparency is almost always a myth in the business world. However, when it comes to building genuine relationships with people, transparency is critical. As the story of Alan Mulally and Ford Motor Company illustrates, a lack of transparency regarding critical business information can act as a cancer within a large organization. You can't solve problems and address issues if you can't see them. Furthermore, we are in an age of unprecedented transparency in terms of access to information. Allow yourself to evolve, grow, and experiment regarding your personal transparency.

THE WORKOUTS

- Honest conversations are important in the workplace. While you can't trust everyone, it is important for your development as a leader that you have at least one person in your workplace you can trust enough to say what you really think in an unvarnished way. Do you have a confidant in whom you can trust and return the favor? If not, cultivate such a relationship.

- When was the last time you admitted a mistake or expressed a concern to your boss? The transformation of Ford Motor Company illustrates the business imperative to operate with the facts. That sounds much easier than it actually is. We all want to appear competent and on top of things. If you can't think of a time when you admitted a mistake, ask yourself whether the reluctance was primarily about you or your boss. Is it fair to assume your boss would have reacted badly, or are you saving face unnecessarily? Or both?

- Get a piece of paper. Take a pencil and draw a line down the middle of the page. Write adjectives that describe the persona you are cultivating on the left side of the page. Write adjectives that you perceive best describe the real you on the other side. Where are the gaps? Mind the gaps carefully.

8

INTERNALIZED MORAL PERSPECTIVE/AN ACTIVE, UNIQUE GPS SYSTEM

Why do you look at the speck that is in your brother's eye, but do not notice the log that is in your own eye? Or how can you say to your brother, "Let me take the speck out of your eye" and behold the log is in your own eye? You hypocrite, first take the log out of your own eye, and then you will see clearly to take the speck out of your brother's eye.
—Matthew 7:3–5, *New American Standard Bible*[1]

I want to show you that an obsession with righteousness (leading inevitably to self-righteousness) is the normal human condition. It is a feature of our evolutionary design, not a bug or error that crept into minds that would otherwise be objective and rational.
—Jonathan Haidt, *The Righteous Mind*[2]

A scorpion and a frog need to cross a river. The frog is obviously better equipped for such a trip, and so the scorpion asks if he can hitch a ride on his back. The frog is afraid of being stung, because he is dealing with a scorpion. Scorpions sting, and the sting would kill the frog. The scorpion argues that if he stings the frog as they're crossing the river, they will both die. In other words, logically, it is not in the best interests of the scorpion to sting the frog. The frog follows the logic and agrees to cross the river with the scorpion riding along.

Halfway through the trip across the river, the scorpion stings the frog. Before they die, the frog asks why. The scorpion famously says, "It is in my nature."

This fable of unknown origins first came to my attention in the 1992 film *The Crying Game*.[3] It is an interesting flick and worth watching if you have not seen it. The film explores both the dark side and the more positive aspects of human nature through the interactions of flawed, complex characters who are all doing what they think is right and/or what they feel compelled to do.

Researchers from diverse disciplines[4,5] have articulated the fourth component of authenticity in psychological terms. That fourth component is behaving in concert or alignment with your values. In order to fully address this piece of the multiple component model, we must delve into the emotionally charged and judgmental territory of morality and ethics.

Developing an internalized sense of right and wrong that is not determined by circumstance and actually behaving in accordance with that value system are two very different things. Our focus in this chapter is about all the ways—large, medium, and small—that we all actually live in concert with our values or fall short every day. It is much easier to let ourselves off the morality hook by talking about the latest terrible thing done by a famous person or a terrorist. Most of us fall somewhere between a terrorist and Mother Teresa in this aspect of authenticity. The old adage "nobody is perfect" applies, as none of us live in concert with our values 24/7. Think of your friend the marathon runner who sneaks a cigarette every now and then. Or maybe that friend is you.

The concept of authenticity is inextricably linked with doing the right things and being a moral person in the real world. All this gets really interesting when we realize that, just like in *The Crying Game*, the world of business and organizations is full of flawed, complex characters who are also doing what they feel is right and/or what they feel compelled to do. It is seductive to think we can easily sort the good people and the bad people. But if we look at the realities of human nature, our own included, it is just not that simple.

Let's do a brief experiment. How do you behave in ways that are consistent and inconsistent with your espoused values? Stop reading! Pause for a minute and process that question. Pay attention to the automatic thoughts that shot through your mind. Get a pen and write down your thoughts in response to the question.

It's likely that your mind responded by thinking about all the people you work with and their inconsistent behaviors while only briefly analyzing your own. That guy in accounting is just awful and doesn't show up half the time. I bet you have a peer who is too pushy and obnoxious. Or perhaps you thought about one of the latest huge moral debacles in the news, such as the Bill Cosby case. And whether you were fully conscious of it or not, you probably were feeling good about the fact that you are generally a good person. Aside from cases of situational guilt or clinical depression, it is in our nature to think, "Of course I am a good person who does the best I can."

When I ask clients to tell me how they behave in ways that are consistent and inconsistent with their values, it takes persistence on my part—bordering on the obnoxious—to get them to admit inconsistencies beyond speeding, working too hard, or not exercising enough. It takes prompting for most of us to think about not exercising as a disconnect between a value on health and actual behavior. We like to think more abstractly about big picture values, obscene behaviors, and morality. Quickly, the conversation turns to the lack of moral behavior on the part of others. This attention to the behavior of others serves to reinforce the idea that all is well on our own moral high ground. As a species, we aren't wired to view ourselves as immoral and don't easily question our own morality. As the eminent social psychologist Jonathan Haidt puts it, "we are all self-righteous." Just as delivering a sting is in the scorpion's nature, being self-righteous is in ours.

We all perceive ourselves to be moral and that the real problem is our colleagues or awful people like Bill Cosby or congressmen who tweet naked photos. Yes, all of us, including you and me. It is literally in our nature to judge the moral behavior of others and find ways to excuse our own shortcomings through a complicated system of justifications. Authentic leadership requires that we prioritize examining our own actions carefully, as opposed to following our nature and paying more attention to the shortcomings of others. In order to be authentic, we must work with and overcome our natural self-righteousness so that we really can live in concert with our values most of the time. I use the metaphor of an active internal GPS system— "active" meaning we have to keep that GPS system turned on and attuned. Making a left turn too early could get you going in a direction you do not want to go, and finding a way to make a U-turn on certain highways can take a long time. Small daily choices make a difference in becoming a more authentic leader and showing up as a better version of yourself.

As it is often said, both God and the devil are in the details. How can you respond authentically and intelligently as you interact with the constant daily pressures that make up your world? We have to ask ourselves whether we are measuring up to our own values on a regular basis and train the mind to actually ponder the question.

In 2007, Bill George completed an exhaustive study of authentic leaders.[6] He focused on the best of the best. The high-performing, authentic leaders in the study all made efforts to be clear about their values and lines that they were unwilling to cross before the pressure hit full force. Knowing and being clear about your values provides a foundation for leading authentically.

But knowing and doing are not the same. George went on to say: "The world may have very different expectations for you and your leadership than you have for yourself. Regardless of whether you are leading a small team or are at the top of a powerful organization, you will be pressured by external forces to respond to their needs and seduced by rewards for fulfilling those needs. It requires courage and resolve to resist the constant pressures and expectations confronting you and to take corrective action when necessary." This chapter provides you with practical psychological and conceptual tools to develop that courage and resolve to stay on track when the heat is on.

It is imperative that authentic leaders be students of human nature in general and experts on the peculiarities of their own particular moral nature. This chapter will get you on the path toward deeper understanding of human nature in general and you in particular. First, we will explore the terrain of human nature through the work of three luminaries in the field of moral psychology. Then, we will dive into the "how" of developing and keeping your own unique internal GPS system activated as you deal with day-to-day pressures.

⸙

PRISONS, ORDERLY STAGES, AND ELEPHANTS

How is that for a section header? In this section, we will walk through the work of three eminent psychologists who have contributed to our understanding of human nature in the moral domain.

The first, Philip Zimbardo, is the iconoclast behind the infamous Stanford Prison Experiment. I have taught the Stanford Prison Experiment to graduate students, undergraduates, and executives. It always makes everyone uncomfortable. In stark contrast, my students like the work of the second psychologist we'll discuss, Lawrence Kohlberg,[7] much better. Kohlberg created logical, orderly stages of moral development that most psychologists can recite. Kohlberg is classic. More recently, Jonathan Haidt[8] has illuminated the more instinctual and intuitive aspects of human nature and characterized the human mind as being like a rider and an elephant. The rider is what you are thinking consciously right now. But that conscious mind (the rider) is on top of a big elephant that represents everything else that is going on right now in you as a person, aside from your to-do list or your frustration with a spouse or coworker who is not living up to his or her values. Somewhere in the vast body of your "elephant," there may already be an instinct taking shape to blow your diet today that your rider has no clue about. According to Haidt, the elephant is 99 percent of your mind, and your top-of-mind automatic consciousness is only 1 percent.

Let's shift gears from thinking about individual consciousness and look at what we can learn about moral psychology from delving into what happens to humans in a prison environment. If you have never volunteered in a prison or visited a prison, I highly recommend it. There is much to be learned about human nature in that setting. The most intense learning experiences of my career occurred when I took a job as a psychologist in the Kentucky Correctional Institution for Women. My motivation was the tuition benefit that the state government was paying. However, working at the prison turned out to be an education in itself. I was 25 years old and saw psychology as a way to make logical sense of the entire universe. In my then-worldview, psychology could add tremendous value to everyone's life. There were no limits, and all people could change if they had the right tools.

My apple cart was quickly upset. First, the warden, Betty Kassulke, informed me that there were many more inmates in KCIW than staff, and my role was to help orchestrate the environment on a psychological level so that we as staff stayed in control and safe. We did not discuss rehabilitation—that is, reintegrating convicted persons into society with the hope that they will not commit crimes again—at length. I brought forth my rehabilitation revelations and Betty nodded as the seasoned do with those who have not dealt with the realities of life just yet. Second, I discovered that staying cool, logical, rational, and removed at all times is not possible in the emotional cauldron of prison.

During the first month, I started to feel unusual emotions of superiority as I walked across the yard in my own clothes while the inmates had to go to their spaces for regular counts. I was the psychologist with my clipboard, nice clothes, and jewelry. With a stroke of a pen I could put an inmate on suicide watch or in solitary confinement. I wrote reports that influenced whether inmates got parole or not. I felt very important, intoxicatingly so, in the world of the Kentucky Correctional Institution for Women. The feelings would start to hit me as I walked through the gates and heard the ominous sounds of the gates clinking. This kind of thing does not usually turn me on. The Stanford Prison Study was starting to resonate with me in a different way than when I had read it in social psychology as both an undergraduate and then later as a graduate student.

In 1971 Philip Zimbardo rocked the world of psychology with his Stanford Prison Experiment. The purpose of the experiment was to understand the development of norms and the effects of roles, labels, and social expectations in a simulated prison environment. I will hit the highlights, but prisonexp.org is an excellent website, if you would like more detail.

Making use of a basement in the psychology building at Stanford, Zimbardo and his team created a prison. He recruited students to play the roles of prisoners and guards for a two-week period of time. Twenty-one males were selected who had been screened for any form of psychopathology, and only those without any such indications were chosen. Hence, all of the volunteers were "normal." The 21 volunteers were randomly assigned to be either prisoners or guards. Every detail of an actual prison was simulated: the uniforms, the counts, the arrests, the removal of personal possessions from the prisoners, and even inmate numbers. It was very much like the realities of prison I witnessed in Kentucky.

The experiment was intended to last two weeks. Zimbardo had to shut it down on the sixth day. In that short amount of time the guards had become abusive toward the inmates, and several inmates were displaying symptoms of psychological distress. Again, the pool of volunteers had been screened for any signs of psychopathology. Furthermore, none of the guards who had behaved so brutally during this time period went to prison for similarly violent behavior after that. They all went on to lead noncriminal lives.

You may be wondering what all of this has to do with your day-to-day realities, which do not involve gates, counts, prisoners, or guards. What does this say about human nature that is relevant to authentic leadership and sticking to your values?

As I discovered working at the prison, our environment powerfully shapes our behavior. There is value in looking at this concept in the vivid, dramatic realities of a prison. I entered the Kentucky correctional facility intending to listen and help, but I quickly got with the program on being strategic about orchestrating the environment to keep us (the staff, my team, and so on) in control. I have never felt such an intoxicating, intense sense of superiority before or after.

There are two takeaways. One, your environment is influencing your behavior in a much more profound way than you likely realize. You are not as independent of it as you think. To be true to your own values, on a practical level you need to be in an organization that closely mirrors those values. To be sure, the pressures in a corporate environment are usually subtler than those in prison. In some ways, subtle pressures are stronger because we may not really see them. I left the prison setting with a briefcase full of important lessons because I did not like who I was becoming in the situation. I was uncomfortable with how good I was getting at spotting a con game and how I was starting to see the world in ways that were not in sync with my values.

Two, if you are in charge of how the environment is set up, pay close attention to detail. How the setup is influencing or shaping human behavior is always a relevant question. For example, there is a trend toward open space in most corporate settings and fewer private offices. This is generally viewed as a good thing. The intention is to decrease the effects of hierarchy and encourage more collaboration. However, one could make the case that you are lowering people's ability to feel separate and think independently just by how you are shaping the environment. Groupthink is a real and valid phenomenon, and there is a sacrifice on the individuality side of the equation when you go into an open-architecture office plan. Furthermore, it might even create more intense feelings of superiority among those chosen few, usually the top leaders, who still have their own offices. Those top leaders may glance at a poster on the wall saying "we value everyone" while feeling very powerful (like me walking into the prison) as they settle into their big office that few people even have anymore. Those feelings of superiority are going to influence their behavior. The only question is how.

In contrast to Zimbardo who upset the apple cart, Lawrence Kohlberg in his years of study as a Harvard professor provided us with a nice, tidy way to order the moral universe. Kohlberg's work is the perennial classic in the field of moral psychology. His stages of moral development are conceptually elegant and create order out of the chaos of figuring out how to navigate complicated moral dilemmas. Over the course of his distinguished career, Kohlberg had thousands of people respond and explain their responses to dilemmas like the following:

A woman was near death from a special kind of cancer. There was one drug that the doctors thought might save her. It was a form of radium that a druggist in the same town had recently discovered. The drug was expensive to make, but the druggist was charging 10 times what the drug *cost him to produce. He paid $200 for the radium and charged $2,000 for a small dose of the drug. The sick woman's husband, Heinz, went to everyone he knew to borrow money. But he could only get $1,000, which was only half the cost. He told the druggist that his wife was dying and asked him to sell it cheaper or let him pay later. But the druggist said no. So Heinz got desperate and broke into the man's laboratory to steal the drug. Should Heinz have broken into the laboratory to steal the drug? Why or why not?*

What is your answer and why? Depending on your answer, you fall into one of the stages of moral development as defined by Kohlberg. There are three general categories called *preconventional, conventional,* and *principle centered.* Each of the three categories has two stages. In Kohlberg's world, it is not important whether you would steal the drug or not. He and his team were listening for the reasons why. The six stages are obedience, self-interest, conformity, law and order, human rights, and universal ethics. The sixth stage is indicative of a higher order of moral development than the third or fourth. So, if you answered that Heinz should not steal the medicine because it is against the law, you are demonstrating stage four. Or if you answered of course he should steal the drug, because saving a human life is more important than the druggist's right to make money from his invention, you would be demonstrating stage six, universal ethics. This stage model gets really interesting when you apply it in the real world. Let me offer you another dilemma I have seen and maybe you have, too.

Brian is a talented consultant and a mover and a shaker in a major global firm who has had a great year and is up for a promotion. His boss, Eric, is also his mentor. The two have similar backgrounds and share a similar set of espoused values with a strong emphasis on family and traditional values. Eric has taught Brian a lot about the business, and they are also friends. Brian knows Eric's wife and children. Brian's primary competitor in the race for the promotion is a woman named Patricia, who is also on Eric's team. Patricia is very good, but Brian believes he is more qualified for the promotion. From the objective HR and talent management point of view, the race for the promotion is very close. Late one night after a team dinner, Brian drives by Patricia's house on his way home and sees Eric's car in the

driveway. He is shocked and then says to himself, "Oh, m
picking something up." The firm has a strict "no sex wit
policy in the ethics code. Brian starts driving by Patricia's ho
at regular intervals. Eric's car is almost always there.

What is an authentic leader who is clear about his values to do?

What is your answer? What would you do? If you choose to let the promotion play out before taking any action whatsoever, Kohlberg would likely put you in stage two, self-interest. If you wanted to display more advanced moral development, stage four, in this situation, you would need to call human resources because Eric's behavior is against the ethical rules of the company. The case of Heinz and stealing the drug seems much more straightforward. Given both Eric and Brian's emphasis on family values, they might agree it was just fine to steal the drug because family is the most important thing in life. They are not as likely to agree on the right response to the affair dilemma. (If you are looking to spice up dinner party conversation and maintain some measure of control, I recommend the Heinz dilemma as opposed to the boss's affair dilemma.)

What insights does Kohlberg's work offer all of us striving to live up to our values? Kohlberg's method and model lends itself well to perspective taking. The order and clarity of the model can open up dialogue about ethical issues and allow people to understand why others tend to be more conventional or rules-centered vs. thinking more about overarching principles. There is tremendous value in perspective taking and being able to look at ethical issues from the point of view of each of the stages. As in most things, acknowledging how you tend to think about things is a value-add, though it is only part of the process that governs ethical or moral behavior.

What is really going on when we behave in concert with the values we say we hold dear? And what is going on when we do not behave in concert with those values—as in the case of Eric, who is family centered and having a secret affair?

The other potent variables that impact ethical decision making are covered in the work of Jonathan Haidt from the Stern School of Business at New York University. Remember Haidt's guiding metaphor of the elephant and the rider. What you are thinking right now is the rider, but there is a lot going on within you that is not so conscious.

In other words, we are all still primates with strong urges and impulses that often override our logical minds; that is, the rider in Haidt's model.

Back to Eric and family values and having an affair with a subordinate. It is not likely that Eric and Patricia started having an affair while either of their riders were calling the shots. The affair is probably not a great idea for either of them on a rational level. Despite the myths of sleeping your way to the top, these things rarely end well for the Patricias of the world, not to mention Eric is taking a profound risk with both his career and personal life.

How is it that such rational, smart people have risky affairs? If I had a chance to interview Eric or Patricia about the affair, it is likely both of them would have very elegant, very smart justifications for their behavior. How does this sound: *As long as no one knows, this affair will not hurt anybody.* Or either of them could say *This is the first real love of my life.* Eric could say *My marriage is over anyway.* Or *We did not mean for this to happen but we fell in love. Out of respect for the firm and Eric's wife, we are keeping this secret.*

Haidt says our riders are essentially lawyers who are really good at justifying the behavior of our elephants. The prefrontal cortex of the human brain (the rider) can justify elephant behavior that is out of sync with values. Hence, according to Haidt, we are all quite self-righteous due to the influence of our inner lawyer. So, Eric and Patricia were attracted to each other on an instinctual level in a flash of strong emotion and commenced an affair. They were enjoying it. The rider had to develop an explanation to justify the affair. *It's true love. Let's keep it a secret and no one will be hurt*, and so on.

How does all of this elephant and rider talk relate to the practicalities of your life as a leader? Like it or not, you too have both an elephant and a rider. Begin to notice how elegantly you can justify an extra scoop of ice cream or fudging on your taxes. We are all really good at rationalizing our behavior, and such justifications are a slippery slope. Once that process begins, the next step gets easier and the lawyer gets smarter. Remember, your attorney's job is not to get to the truth, but to argue your case. That is how intelligent people like Patricia and Eric, who have every intention of living their values, wind up having secret affairs.

Next, the lawyers of other people in the situation, like Brian, use their lawyers to judge Eric and Patricia. Brian might say their behavior is against the principles of the firm. *What are they thinking?* Or what about the principle of telling the truth? Remember, Kohlberg's highest stages are about living according to universal principles like truth telling. Brian's lawyer can reel all this off like a well-argued brief. Not to mention the arguments about wrongdoing on all of Kohlberg's levels that Eric's wife could likely argue with passion. Or how about human resources?

PUTTING UP PSYCHOLOGICAL GUARDRAILS

I was planning an executive offsite with a very savvy senior vice president of human resources. The focus of the offsite was to clarify the key values of a new company that had formed as a result of the merger of equals. Our task was to define a list of values and then talk through how to drive them throughout the new organization. We walked through the design and the VP said: "I have a question. What are the guardrails? In other words, how do we identify it quickly when we as individuals or as a team are getting off track?" The team was already getting good at justifying all kinds of behaviors, she said, and they'd only been a team for a few months.

In other words, this astute executive had already heard all the "lawyers" (the chief counsel included) on the executive team justifying things that the inner elephants wanted to do. In this section, we will cover psychological guardrails. The guardrails include practical watch-outs for you, and behaviors that will help you cultivate inner strength as you pay more attention to the small, medium, and large ways you either live your values, and less attention to the seductive, dramatic reality show of other people.

The first guardrail is *The Wall Street Journal* test. One of the most ethical executives I have ever worked with hit a rough patch in his career over a six-word e-mail. One of his employees had accepted a vendor's offer to pay for a weekend in Napa Valley. The e-mail from the employee was essentially a request that the same vendor's annual cap be increased by $100,000. According to the e-mail, the request had been made during a delightful weekend at a vineyard with the vendor as the host. My client e-mailed back six words: "What the [blank] are you thinking?" The employee took the six-word e-mail to human resources and complained, and a whole drama ensued about both the curse word in the e-mail and the violation of the vendor policy, which wasn't in either person's best interests.

The employee wound up getting fired. When the employee went to HR, it reminded me of the scorpion and the frog. Was backstabbing just in this guy's nature or something? In conversation with my highly ethical (but prone to using curse words) client, I said, "From now on don't write anything into an e-mail that you would not want in *The Wall Street Journal.*" Over the years, I have come to call it *The Wall Street Journal* test. I would say the same applies for social media.

You don't want your entire life to revolve around *The Wall Street Journal* test, of course. Some measure of privacy is allowable and fair. You need zones of safety and people you can trust in your life. However, if you feel the impulse to hide something from trustworthy people whose opinions you typically value, take note. You may be on the slippery slope of secrecy, self-justification, and self-righteousness.

The second guardrail is a simple exercise that works with both individuals and teams. It is a simple directive: "Give me an example." Let's say as an individual you value being honest with your colleagues and saying what you really think about business issues. This is difficult for you, as you grew up in a family where everything was made to look just great, but it was actually a big mess. Challenge yourself weekly to first write down an example in which you fudged the truth or where you did not live up to your value of telling colleagues the truth in a clear manner. Then, give yourself two examples where you did live up to the value.

The same process works with teams. Have individuals on the team respond to the same two directives. The 1:2 ratio is important, as is reporting out either to colleagues in a team setting, yourself, or a coach. The way the exercise is set up forces you out of self-righteous mode by confessing where you did not measure up first. Then, balancing that out with examples of where you did measure up puts you in a different state. If working in a team, you can also have your colleagues debate such examples, as everyone perceives a situation a little differently.

In an extension of "give me an example," I encourage leaders to share examples and stories in public forums of real people throughout the organization living the values. Leaders need to constantly look for opportunities to connect the dots between the ideas of the values and the actual behaviors. This becomes a way to train everyone's brain to connect the dots as well. For example, a senior leader commending an employee by name who brought a safety problem to the attention of management is more powerful than 1,000 safety lectures.

Third, challenge yourself and your team to keep it real and avoid grandiosity in any values or mission statement. Avoid vague statements like "making the world a better place" in expressing your team or organization's values. The HBO show *Silicon Valley* [9] is a parody of the peculiarities of the Internet start-up world of the U.S. West Coast. The storyline follows a young geek with a big idea and his company named Pied Piper. Pied Piper eventually becomes sought after in the larger Silicon Valley culture. The management team crafts its own mission statement, which reads, in a hilarious twist: "Pied Piper isn't some bloated corporation with a pretentious mission statement about making the world a better place. We hope to positively impact our planet."

Seriously, these vague statements emanate from an intention to be motivational. However, you don't often come across one of these statements that influences behavior on a daily basis. The familiar wall hangings risk becoming a source of cynicism, as opposed to inspiration.

⧬

THE ONE THING

The epigraphs at the beginning of the chapter from Jesus and Jonathan Haidt essentially communicate the same message in very different ways. In the Sermon on the Mount, Jesus said, "Why are you looking at the speck in your colleague's eye when you have a log in your own eye?" When I memorized the Bible verse as a child, I found the very idea of having a log in your eye to be hilarious. The implications, however, can be far more serious when people in powerful roles have logs in their eyes. Jonathan Haidt's work has clarified that we do have a built-in perceptual error when it comes to facing and making sense of our own moral and ethical behavior. This log in our eye is fundamental to how we see ourselves in the world. It takes constant vigilance on the part of leaders to remain true to their values. You cannot trust that internal sense that of course you are a good person. The one thing leaders can never do is feel they have arrived at a place in which they are living their values and stop asking the hard questions. The work is never done. You must keep your internal GPS active.

❦

THE WORKOUTS

- Courage is a strength you will need as you try to live your values under pressure. How does one cultivate courage? Check out this advice from *Character Strengths Matter: How to Live a Full Life*, edited by Shannon Polly and Kathryn Britton:[10] "Pretend as if you have a strength. Act as if you are courageous and brave." There are many applications of this advice. I often break it down for my clients by assigning them to act as though they are courageous for one meeting or one day. Then, we debrief the lessons learned. What exactly did they do differently or the same when they were acting as if they were brave? The key is to keep the acting as if top of mind for the entire meeting or the entire day.

- Challenge yourself to give examples of your own behaviors in regard to a specific value in the 1:2 ratio described in this chapter for one week. Notice how doing the exercise impacts your behavior. Paradoxically, in owning up to your own misbehaviors, you are training yourself to behave more ethically. Think about it: Organized religion came up with the idea of confession a long time ago.

- Identify someone you admire in your organization for living out the values of the company in a real way. Proactively connect with that person and get to know them at a deeper level through a simple coffee meeting. Intentionally work with and surround yourself with people you admire for living out their values as much as possible. Who we interact with on a routine basis heavily affects our own behaviors.

PART III

THE MASTER CLASS

9

THE CENTRALITY OF CONSCIOUS CHOICE

We have the ability to create choice by altering our interpretations of the world.

—Sheena Iyengar, *The Art of Choosing*[1]

I settled into my back jack, well into the post-lunch mental haze and downright sleepiness that often accompany weeklong training sessions. Why was I using a back jack as opposed to sitting like a civilized person in a conference room? Furthermore, what exactly *is* a back jack? Think of it like a meditation cushion, but with a modicum of back support. I was in the middle of what was called the "immersion" in the yearlong Certificate in Positive Psychology (CIPP) program at Kripalu. Kripalu is the largest yoga center in North America. If you go to a learning program in the main hall at Kripalu, you won't find a traditional setup. You won't see big round tables with chairs and table tents like in a big meeting room at a hotel. And it does not look like an

MBA classroom, either. You are more likely to see people sitting on the floor and they may have blankets while listening to what looks like a traditional lecture, except the speaker is usually barefoot. The faculty of the CIPP had envisioned a program bringing together the scientific rigor of positive psychology and the disciplined inquiry into mind and body that comprises yoga.

On a more personal level, what had started out as a quest for continuing education credits was quickly turning into a transformative experience for cynical old me. We did a brief stretch and meditation practice that helped me tune in a bit. Then, Tal Ben-Shahar, the renowned positive psychologist, stood up, took a deep breath, and said, "You always have a choice, even if it is just to breathe deeply."

You know how sometimes something really hits you like a bolt of lightning? Ben-Shahar's words struck me that way. I am a psychologist and could go on and on about the power of choice in the abstract. But what hit me that day at a level below the intellect is the power of the perception of choice. Not just choice, but the *perception* of choice. Think about it: In almost any situation, you still have the choice to breathe deeply. Yes, in some life-threatening situations, oxygen may be scarce, but you get the point. It is likely that any time on any day in your work environment, you always have the choice to breathe deeply, which at the very minimum will calm you down and keep you from having a panic attack.

If you think this whole choice thing is easy, though, try to remember to breathe deeply at work. Choices to manage oneself in such ways are simple, but not easy to remember when your team is totally dysfunctional and missing an important deadline. But we will get into that later.

I work every day with people in leadership roles. They make business choices every day alone and with others that have huge consequences: Should we shut down that plant? Does it make sense to make an acquisition now? Shall I hire this person or not? But what about the choices we all make about who to be as a person? How much choice and power do my clients feel to actually shape themselves in terms of day-to-day behavioral choices? Furthermore, how does choice connect to authentic leadership?

DEBUNKING POPEYE'S VERSION OF AUTHENTICITY

Popeye, the Sailor Man was a popular Saturday morning cartoon when I was a kid. If you are of a certain age with me, you may remember. Popeye was known for two things: eating spinach and declaring "I yam what I yam!" with absolute certainty. Of course, that translates to "I am what I am," which is the lazy leader's view of authenticity—especially when we don't want to put forth a lot of effort to deal with an aspect of ourselves intentionally and skillfully.

Marcus, one of my most talented and intellectually voracious clients, gave me a modern "I am what I am" speech a while back. He had recently moved into a new position and asked me to do a check-in with his team regarding overall team dynamics. He had been in the new position for about six months, and the vast majority of his team remarked that they did *not* feel that they knew Marcus any better than they did when he showed up.

This was surprising to me, as Marcus's team in his former position had described him as the most caring manager they'd ever had. Also, while his new team delivered exceptional business results, they reported morale was only "so-so." There is a natural human tendency to feel more positive when you are winning, so it was noteworthy that morale was just so-so. Thinking longer term, how would the team weather a storm in which the business performance was not so good? Every business has challenging periods. The practical reason for building team morale is to help deal with those challenging times.

A few people remarked that they missed their former leader. I brought up this finding with Marcus and he said, "You know, Karissa, I have been trying to step a bit more out of the detail." As we continued our discussion he enthusiastically explained that "ever since reading Susan Cain's book, *Quiet: The Power of Introverts in a World That Can't Stop Talking,*[2] I have come to believe that my natural introversion is a gift, and maybe I've been faking it all these years in my interactions with people."

At such moments, my "I am what I am" first thought is *Are you crazy?*

I had read Cain's excellent book as well, but Marcus's interpretation of the book did not take into account the specifics of the leadership challenge in front of him, nor his deeply held values and goals. However, I chose to take a very pregnant pause and look him in the eye with my glasses on my nose. Then, he started backing up and asking a whole bunch of specific questions about the data. I eventually asked Marcus how his newfound mode of behaving according to his introversion and shutting his door more often (not necessarily a bad thing, but remember I know Marcus and his organization well) jived with the guy whose last team experienced him as the most caring manager they had ever had. Was the caring fake, too?

That one got a strong reaction! "Of course not; I did not fake caring," he said adamantly. Do you not care for this team? Do you not like them? In one conversation we moved Marcus from "I am what I am" to "I am what I choose." This is not a one-time thing for any of us. We have to choose to choose over and over, and it does take effort.

Let's step back from Marcus's story for a moment and think about it. His natural state was to be introverted, but in his former position he had chosen to push himself to be more open and inviting to his team. After reading *Quiet*, Marcus interpreted that openness as though he was sacrificing something (a sellout) and not being his true self. Over several conversations, Marcus realized that doing something that did not come naturally to him was not necessarily inauthentic if he chose the behavior based on one of his core values. Those less comfortable behavioral choices that come from deeply held values can actually serve to make leaders more authentic over time.

Becoming more authentic over time is a fundamental choice for leaders. Psychological research has much to offer about how to shape yourself in desired ways. But it's not magic, and it's not easy. Cynicism is a strong force, and despite our culture of self-help, many of us will admit it is difficult to change and shape ourselves. We have all failed at it to some degree. My clients are often shocked that, yes, they really can listen more effectively, or be more strategic, or grow as an authentic leader.

First, you must clarify in your own mind and heart that becoming more authentic and real is your goal. You must commit to the process, which as we covered in Part 2 includes cultivating selves awareness, balanced processing, relational transparency, and an internalized moral compass. The components of psychological authenticity are based in science. Bringing those components to life in demanding situations is an art. In Part 3 we move beyond the basics and into the master class on psychological authenticity. The term "master class" is borrowed from the world of music. In a master class, the expert musician takes one student at a time and listens to his or her performance. This format allows an advanced student to refine and hone skills. Section 3 is about refining and honing your skills as an authentic leader.

We begin with the most important concept: the centrality of choice.

❧

THE REALITY OF AUTHENTICITY

Making conscious choices and owning your own life is at the heart of the art of authenticity. The choice to become a more authentic leader over time is the big, fundamental choice that impacts all of your other choices. Israeli scholars Boas Shamir and Gamit Eilam[3] effectively argue that being a leader is a central aspect of the way authentic leaders view themselves.

Take it one step further and say the goal of being an authentic leader becomes central to your view of who you want to be. Thus, the desire to be an authentic leader impacts small, medium, and large choices. Authenticity is not an abstract, feel-good concept, but a filter through which you view real-time choices. We are all the sum total of our choices. This chapter is about encouraging you to be more aware of your choices in regard to managing yourself that you make every day as a leader, some of them conscious and many others on autopilot.

Authenticity is not simply "being yourself." As you have discovered in Part 2 and probably already knew, you are not that simple. Real-world authenticity is fundamentally a process of self-invention, creation, and ongoing self-shaping based on interactions with all kinds of situations. We often fall into false dichotomies. For example, we can either conform to the demands of a situation *or* be ourselves. The challenge of authenticity requires you to think differently and step out of that false dichotomy. I have worked with many people over the years who see themselves as a sellout and dream of leaving their organization to start a nonprofit due to the impact of this false dichotomy. They feel like they are just selling clothes, toilet paper, or yogurt. Where's the meaning in that?

When I begin to probe, I discover that many of them are actually doing great things right where they are. They enjoy the process of figuring out a market, and that is an authentic expression of who they are. Or they have found a way to exploit a new opportunity in an established business, which creates whole new divisions of the company. Such folks have not changed the world in the way they imagined in their youth, but they are making a positive impact in various ways. Dichotomous thinking is a trap that can hinder our effectiveness and our well-being.

❧

Choosing Authentic Action

The alternative to the false dichotomies that are so prevalent is to broaden your mind-set on the concept of authenticity by incorporating systems theory. The basic idea in systems theory is that all parts of a system interact and affect one another. For example, if you have a fight-or-flight stress reaction in your body, it is initiated in your nervous system, but it affects every other organ in your body.

How exactly does systems theory relate to authenticity? (My clients have trained me well by using the "how exactly" phrase when I get too psychological! Or better yet, "Karissa what are you trying to tell me?") The action of authenticity is in the interaction. Authentic action takes into account both who you are and the situation, not one at the expense of the other. The key is to figure out actions that take into account both who you are and the situational demands.

Once you begin to zoom out and think about it in this way, you will see that there are several options for authentic action in many situations. You have choice. Authentic action can be choosing to conform to demands or pushing back. It can also demand creative thinking and coming up with a third or fourth way that is not exactly conforming and not exactly pushing back. Authentic action takes into account both you and the situation.

For example, I was retained to work with a client named Robert, whose boss, Tim, viewed him as extremely talented. The concern was that senior leaders had no idea who he was because Robert had only had brief social interactions with the higher-ups. In fact, when Robert's boss extolled how great he was, the higher-ups weren't quite sure who he was talking about. Robert had committed the unpardonable sin of not making an impression.

As I got to know Robert, I realized that social interaction was not his forte. No amount of coaching was going to make this guy shine at the cocktail hour. He was very serious and task focused. If Robert's boss was right and the company needed his expertise, how could we make him more visible? I asked Tim if there was an opportunity for an intense, pressure-filled project assignment that would involve working directly with specific higher-ups that really mattered. He sharply barked at me that he was working on one right now—but had shielded Robert from it. "If Robert can't connect socially," he said, "I'm concerned he'll make the wrong impression." I pushed back, pointing out that Robert did have a history of connecting socially after he'd worked intensively with people. I noted a few examples. I recommended that we put Robert on the project immediately, with his boss maintaining some contact.

Robert did make a positive impression and actually took charge in an impressive way when the project started to derail. This story has a happy ending, as it worked to give Robert the visibility he needed. But his social comfort is not much different even though he is now at a higher level. Robert would still prefer a root canal to a cocktail party. However, he understands that the interaction is important and does his best. Both he and his boss were stuck in a false dichotomy that was not helping Robert be more authentic or effective. His boss was saying socialize and Robert was not doing it. Robert never became a cocktail party star, but he did learn to open up to people through self-deprecating comments about his intensity delivered with humor.

Ironically, the later version of Robert was actually more approachable than many highly extroverted cocktail party stars. He was able to use his keen listening skills to understand people just as deeply as he understood business issues.

In the journey toward being more authentic, all of us go through many different versions of ourselves. Authenticity is a call to actively shape those versions and be self-authoring and intentional, as opposed to being shaped by circumstance. The rest of the chapter will provide you with guidance and tools useful in the daily process of choosing to become an authentic leader and your best self (or a grander version of who you already are).

My only problem with the term "best self" is that it sounds final. This work is by its very nature always iterative, like science. And just like science, experiments enable the learning.

⚜

CHOOSE TO EXPERIMENT

I can predict how successful an executive coaching gig is going to be within the first month, and if we'll have wild success within the first two weeks. By wild success I mean that the engagement is a meaningful learning experience for the individual and that he or she has improved on a key leadership skill of value to the organization. One without the other would not qualify as a wild success.

You might assume that as long as the leader seems motivated and willing, we're set for wild success. (Remember the old lightbulb joke: How many psychologists does it take to change a lightbulb? Answer: One, if the lightbulb is willing.) But I've worked with eager, willing participants who claimed mediocre results at best.

Executive coaching will be wildly successful if—and only if—my new client chooses to experiment with at least one new behavior within the first two weeks. No experiments in process during the first two weeks, no wild success.

As Herminia Ibarra has clearly articulated in *Act Like a Leader, Think Like a Leader*,[4] there is a good deal of research making it clear that moving into action is the best way to initiate any kind of change process. Acting differently often precedes thinking and feeling differently. This is especially true with executives who tend to be action-oriented by nature. So, when my clients jump in and experiment, we are doing more than a simple experiment. They are beginning a process that is likely to broaden who they are as leaders. Aspects of self that they have not been bringing to the role will likely join the party as we move along.

This whole self-broadening process needs to start as soon as possible to make wild success achievable. Each client is strongly encouraged from the first meeting to try something new, even if it is small. I use the term "behavioral experiment" and I say some will work, some will not, and other experiments will be neutral in your view. The most important thing is that you experiment and try something new.

In order to qualify as an experiment, the behavior has to be easily measurable. There can be no murky gray area regarding whether you did it or not. Here are typical examples: saying no to three meetings a day, calling as opposed to e-mailing a person you do not like and are fighting with, or practicing power poses before a presentation to pump yourself up. The experiments are customized to the individual's constitution, situation, the organization, and are based in the science of psychology. Tailoring the experiment to the situation, organization, and person is my job. There is no "maybe" as to whether or not these experiments in authentic leadership development are completed or not. The client either completes the experiment or does not.

Let's take power poses as an example. Amy Cuddy's research has clearly demonstrated that people who hold themselves in powerful positions prior to and during anxiety-provoking situations perform more effectively. See Cuddy's TED Talk, "Your Body Language Shapes Who You Are,"[5] for more detail. When the client says to me, "I practiced those power poses and I think it helped," I know we are on the road to success. A massive debriefing follows, consisting of several questions. Just like the scientific method, we study the results with this sample of one, identify key lessons, and suggest future experiments.

We are also on the road to success if my client says, "I tried those power poses, and it didn't work." That requires its own debriefing. How did you think it would work? What happened instead? What might have helped more? What else was going on that day? When do you feel powerful and confident? Essentially, we go through the same general process whether the client views the experiment as a success or not. Either way, the client has another experiment to conduct after the meeting. The magic of change takes place in the doing and then reflecting on the doing, and then doing some more.

Our ultimate goal is "reflaction" or reflection in action. Working with me is a series of experiments. Then, I reflect with the clients about whether the experiments worked or not. One of the important questions after every experiment is, how did the new behavior feel to you? Can you see yourself doing it again? Why or why not? What part of you were you expressing? These questions get at *felt authenticity*. Felt authenticity is that sense that you are being yourself or, more accurately, your selves. Developmental psychologist Susan Harter[6] observes in her work that we are much more conversant and aware in our culture of what feels or looks false. We attach more mystery to authenticity. We are not sure what authenticity is, but we know it when we see it. I encourage my clients to develop their own internal self-barometers of fakeness and authenticity through skillful self inquiry.

One of the important habits of authentic leaders is to build that barometer. As you do, you are likely to notice that felt fakeness drains your energy and felt authenticity tends to raise your energy. Interestingly enough, very few of the experiments feel false to my clients. It is much more common for clients to say they did not get the results they envisioned in doing the experiment.

If my clients, who are skilled leaders, do not consider the experiments inauthentic, then why do they not think of them on their own? (With all due respect to the coach, the experiments are not rocket science.) This brings us to another choice on the journey of authentic leadership development.

✌

CHOOSE TO NOTICE THE NOVEL

It was finally my turn in line at the busy Chipotle in Rehoboth Beach. Chipotle is a fast casual dining spot that has grown exponentially in the United States in recent years. As a customer you get to customize your burrito and watch as it is being made. It is real food and is part of the trend toward freshness. Most important, it's a very tasty lunch. I tell the person behind the counter I want a chicken fajita burrito, no rice. She asks what kind of rice I'd like, white or brown. I again say, "No rice." She stands there holding the ladle in the rice and again says "rice" with a question in her body language. I say louder and with emphasis, "*No rice.*" She looks terrified and removes the ladle. Why was the Chipotle worker terrified of the customer who did not want rice?

That brings us to the work of renowned psychologist Ellen Langer[7] on scientific mindfulness. The worker at Chipotle did not have a category in her mind for a rice-less burrito eater. *Categorical thinking* helps us all get things done every day. However, it also keeps us from noticing and reacting to the novel in everyday situations. Or, as Langer would say, most of us are just not there. We are mindless and on autopilot most of our days. It takes effort on our part to really show up and be present. Langer's approach to mindfulness is based in cognitive science.

Meditation is one way to create a mindful state, but there are many other ways. For example, one of my clients was spending a lot of time in her boss's office. This was not a good thing in her situation. They kept having similar circuitous conversations regarding why costly mistakes were continuing to happen on a key project and that something must be done. The two of them were locked into a negative pattern of having the same conversation and my client not feeling comfortable doing anything they had discussed. My client felt like her boss did not really get what was going on and her boss felt like she did not really understand the long-term implications of these mistakes. I asked her to notice three new things either in the office or about her boss every time she was in the office for the meetings. At first, she looked at me like that worker from Chipotle, terrified and wondering if I was a little off. But she agreed to give it a try. Sure enough, when she moved into a more mindful state, her boss followed suit and ultimately, the two of them were able to find common ground in the midst of a project from hell.

Mindlessness is essentially an inactive state of mind with a reliance on categories that either made sense in the past or make sense for a percentage of the situations you face. The following conditions categorize Langer's mindless state:

- The past overpowers the present
- One narrow perspective dominates
- Insensitivity to context
- Rule and routine governed

Mindlessness is easier than cognitive mindfulness. When I tell executive teams "if you want to be an effective team, make every interaction with your team members a conscious choice," they are intrigued at first. How hard can this really be? Then, they try it and admit it's exhausting. Becoming more mindful at work is an important discipline for authentic leaders. You have to work at it. In contrast to mindlessness, mindfulness is characterized by:

1. The creation of new categories
2. Rule and routine guided
3. Openness to new information
4. Emotional alertness and engagement

On a practical level, how does one cultivate mindfulness as opposed to mindlessness? It is easy to see the benefits of being mindful but difficult to remember once you get in the heat of the day with 108 e-mails and eight meetings and the pressure to get several things done in an unreasonable time frame.

A regular three-minute time-out is helpful. Try this: Put an alarm on your phone or iPad and schedule a three-minute time-out at 10 AM, 2 PM, and 4 PM. During the time-out, you are alone. Take a couple of deep breaths and ask yourself, how is the day going? What have I noticed today that was unique? Even seemingly insignificant things can help keep you in a mindful state. Examples might include a colleague's suntan or bad mood. You may notice that the art in the office is really terrible. Many of my clients need a challenge, so I ask them to write down what they have noticed that was unique and send it to me. It quickly turns into a competition to notice more, which if not taken too far, serves our goal.

❧

In Closing

Tennis legend Andre Agassi's 2009 autobiography, *Open*,[8] is a story about the power of the perception of choice in big and small ways. Agassi chose to experiment constantly. He experimented with versions of self in visible ways and continued to experiment and take risks to improve his game. He also demonstrates a natural tendency toward Langer's mindfulness. According to Langer, high performers in every discipline are mindful in terms of being attuned and noticing the novel. Finally, there is always dissonance as Agassi strives to be more.

Agassi discloses in his autobiography that he has actually hated tennis for most of his life. Tennis was a choice his father made for him when he was a young boy. As a result, for many years as an adult, he did not perceive that he had a choice. His talent, along with his father's motivation to have a son who was a professional tennis player, propelled him to the top when he was young. But he rose to a whole other level of greatness when he *chose* tennis as an adult in his thirties and became the oldest man ever ranked number one. Agassi's inspirational journey includes falling from the top to the bottom and climbing back again. He struggled with motivation and purposelessness midcareer before finding himself and cultivating a more mature sense of purpose, including using his celebrity to provide educational opportunities for kids in his hometown of Las Vegas. His autobiography is a story of a person making the choice to become more authentic over time. Becoming more authentic is not a straight line but one filled with challenges, struggles, and mistakes. The seasoned tennis philosopher and philanthropist that is Agassi today bears little resemblance to the brash kid with all the hair that starred in the "image is everything" campaign in 1990. Agassi writes:

> It's no accident, I think, that tennis uses the language of life. Advantage, service, fault, break, love, the basic elements of tennis are those of everyday existence, because every match is a life in miniature. Even the structure of tennis, the way the pieces fit inside one another like Russian nesting dolls, mimics the structure of our days. Points become games become sets become tournaments, and it's all so tightly connected that any point can become the turning point. It reminds me of the way seconds become hours, and any hour can be our finest. Or darkest. It's our choice.

The ball is in your court. Serve it up. Choose to choose.

⚜

THE WORKOUTS

- Play with the following three questions next time you are in a situation at work that you find stressful. Our mind-sets become extremely narrow and mindlessness is easy to slip into when we're under high stress.

- ○ How would you describe this situation to someone from a small village in Africa?

- ○ How would you describe this situation to an eight-year-old?

- ○ How would everyone respond if you stood up and screamed at the top of your lungs? (Don't actually do this!)

- Begin to build your authenticity barometer. Identify two important interactions in the next week. It could be a presentation or a team meeting in which you have to share results that you wish were better. After the interaction, quantify on a scale of 1–10: How authentic did you feel? What choices did you make that created a sense of felt authenticity or not? Developing this barometer is powerful in your journey toward becoming more authentic.

- Choose to experiment. Do something different as soon as possible. It can be as simple as taking a walk around the building during lunch. Our patterns and routines serve us, but we do not want to become mental slaves to them. Disrupt your pattern by doing something different on a physical level. We started this chapter with me in a back jack, which is strikingly different from the traditional office setup. While I don't recommend a back jack, it is useful to do something different like sitting on the floor or stretching as you are thinking about a problem. Disrupting your typical physical pattern can broaden your mind-set. Taking a different route to work that was actually longer helped one of my clients solve a longstanding operational problem that was costing a lot of money.

10

HOW TO READ CULTURE LIKE AN ANTHROPOLOGIST

People's BS detectors are finely tuned when it comes to corporate speak;
they can tell when you don't mean it. So when you put your mission in
writing, it had better be authentic. A good litmus test is to ask what
would happen if you change the statements that describe culture.
—Eric Schmidt and Jonathan Rosenberg[1]

I picked up my iPhone to find a frantic HR executive, Katherine, on the other end of the line. Katherine explained that the executive team was split between two potential candidates for the chief information technology role in the company.

I had been serving as an advisor and assessor of talent while Katherine recruited executives in an effort to build a new executive team. The current company was the result of the merger of two different companies. We had been actively trying to recruit people who were not from either of the legacy companies as well as intentionally retaining key people from both legacy companies who were judged to be a good fit with the vision for the new company.

Katherine and I had spoken regularly for several weeks, but I had never heard her so frantic. Come to find out, the president had been clear with Katherine that the CTO should have been hired by now. The temporary CTO's energy was waning, and in the president's opinion he wasn't that good anyway.

Katherine went on to say that while she thought both of the potential candidates would make a good match for the position, each candidate seemed to elicit strong reactions from various individuals on the executive team. The executive team had divided into polarized camps like Democrats and Republicans, with one faction supporting candidate A, and the other faction supporting candidate B. Katharine articulated our challenge: We needed to choose the candidate who would make the best fit for both the culture of the organization they were still in the process of creating and the culture of the executive team.

Immediately, I started accessing my ignorance and practicing what Edgar Schein[2] calls *humble inquiry*. Looking at this as a simple choice between two people and hence two factions on the executive team was a seductive trap I had no desire to fall into. It could be a lucrative gig for me, but I could actually make the situation worse if I did not help the client see the issue from a broader cultural lens.

⚮

Practical Anthropology Via iPhone

I asked Katherine a lot of questions—who is siding with whom? Are the factions of equal size? Is anyone staying neutral? What does this disagreement on the team look like, and how does it play out? Does it play out with everyone in the room, or are there sidebar conversations that are influencing things? How are the outsiders (people who do not come from either legacy company) reacting to the disagreement? Has anyone changed factions yet?

Hiring decisions are not simple for the organization hiring or for the person making the choice to come to work in any organization. At the senior level in particular, bad hires are costly. You are looking for someone who is a fit for the culture, but also someone who can make good things happen in the context of the culture and potentially shape that culture to be even more effective. At the individual level, working in a place that is a bad fit can be a real downer, especially if it is your first job out of college.

Katherine got my point. Unless we took the time to understand the behavior and culture of the executive team at a deeper level, our project would likely fail. Failure often sounds like "that did not work because he or she was a bad cultural fit" but nobody knows exactly what they mean by that. Something mysteriously did not work. But it is really not that mysterious. Back to Katherine and her dilemma.

Let's say one group on the executive team wins, and its preferred candidate becomes the new chief technology officer. How likely is the other faction to support that candidate? A broader lens than winning and losing was required to resolve the dilemma. This disagreement was an opportunity for the team to examine its own culture and have a clearer view of what they were creating during the early days of a merger.

Culture starts to form pretty quickly when you put a group of people together. My job as a consultant was to help those leaders be intentional about the culture they were creating as opposed to allowing human nature to simply take its course. Culture will happen.

It is almost impossible to articulate the particulars of the culture in which you live every day. Fish have a hard time describing water. (I know fish don't speak, but you get my point.) Edgar Schein, a professor emeritus at the MIT Sloan School of Management, has been the thought leader in developing a way of working and thinking with clients informed by anthropology that lends itself well to organizations. Simply put, anthropology is the study of people, past and present. Anthropologists use the terms *rites* and *rituals* in their studies. Organizations have rituals, or ways of doing things, that become habits and become ingrained in the organization over time. The way meetings are conducted is an example of a ritual. Rituals or habits are powerful determinants of human behavior.

At one time, I did a lot of consulting at a small nuclear power plant. The plant ran into some issues that were of concern to the Nuclear Regulatory Commission that involved a lack of cross-functional alignment. The plant manager implemented a 6:30 AM meeting every day, seven days a week, in which operations, engineering, and health physics (the people who keep us all safe) met in the same room and discussed everything that was happening in the next 24 hours. That 6:30 meeting, held every day no matter what, was the ritual that dealt with the issues. No one was yelled at. But everyone in the key functions communicated regularly as a result of the artful intervention of the plant manager. All he did was mandate the meeting. The culture was such that if the plant manager mandated a meeting, it happened. He personally attended for a few months. Then, he trusted his team to carry on with the ritual.

The term *rites* usually refers to things that are more ceremonial, such as a bar mitzvah or a baptism. You can see organizational rites in things like holiday celebrations or what happens when people make partner in a professional services firm. The rites and rituals in modern corporations may be less obvious than the rites and rituals of a remote tribe in Africa, but be not deceived: The rites and rituals in modern organizations are just as powerful in directing human behavior.

The organizational culture in which you work is affecting you in ways you are aware of and ways you are not aware of. I brought the perspective of an outsider into the mix for this pressure-filled situation. When Katherine called, her expectation was that I would complete psychological assessments on both candidates and, as an expert, deliver a verdict regarding which candidate was better. Then, due to my expert view, the executive team would get on board. Then, the president of the division would be off her back.

That plan would not have worked.

Luckily for us all, I've grown smarter through the years. Only through investigative dialogue with skillful outsiders and willing insiders can the culture actually be excavated. It often does feel a bit like I imagine an archaeological dig feels. You are never quite sure when you are going to hit on something important, but everyone in the discussion seems to light up when you get there. The simplest and best way to think about culture is simply the way things are done over and over again by a specific group of people. Put three or more people together and as they develop habits of doing and interacting, you have a culture.

After that conversation, I talked with several other executive team members and put together a document that clarified exactly what we were looking for in the IT executive. The document had leadership competencies like driving change, finding ways to cut the budget—particularly in IT architecture—but spend money on upgrades that would enable salespeople to provide customers real-time information, and developing teams.

The document also had softer things, like a willingness to collaborate until all key stakeholders could agree on the decision at the executive level. I used the way I was brought into the mix as an example. I pointed out that most executive teams do not require that everyone agree and feel good about a person before a new executive is brought on to the team. In our cultural dig, that was a big finding. We needed a CTO who could tolerate and perhaps value a team in which everyone needed to feel good about whom they invited into their ranks. I asked them about other teams they had been a part of and how hiring had worked.

Many executive teams would have simply pulled the trigger based on the recommendation of the hiring committee. Not this team. The culture of the executive team mandated that every member fully support every other member. The living of that value began when a new member was being considered for the team. They were also trying to live out a culture in which every team member's viewpoint mattered.

Wondering how the drama of which IT executive to hire played out? One of the two candidates pulled himself out of the running because he perceived that in a culture that required that much discussion to make a decision, he would not be able to get anything done. Not a good fit for him! In discussion with him, he related that he would feel fake if he tried to slow down to operate in such an environment and definitely frustrated. In short, he did not feel he could be authentic in the culture. We assessed the remaining candidate with a sharp eye toward the list of competencies and cultural dimensions teased out of our discussions. The candidate was selected and given feedback.

He was generally a good fit and has since been successful in the organization. However, he credits the clarity with which the culture was explained to him through the hiring process to have been extremely helpful as he adjusted to the new work environment. He said he usually had to figure all of that out on his own.

To his point, the way things really work are rarely explained to new recruits in clear terms. That can be problematic in creating success and also in becoming a more authentic leader. It is easy to find yourself in a bad fit that seemed like such a good fit on paper and during the interview process.

⬥⬥⬥

IS THE ORGANIZATION WORKING TO BE MORE AUTHENTIC?

In becoming more authentic, your choice of the culture in which to work matters. It will most certainly shape you. And if you understand the culture, you have a shot at helping to shape it. You cannot become more authentic in a culture that is generally not in sync with your values. On the flip side, you can grow in ways you would not have thought possible in the right fit for you. It is critical to be in a place that is generally in sync with your values and who you are. You can grow even if the culture is not a 100 percent perfect fit. Perfection in terms of fit rarely happens.

Some organizations genuinely work to live out their values and be authentic at the organizational level—and others simply don't value being authentic or for real in that way. You can't assume what people say is for real. Even the organizations that are working at it aren't perfect—just like us as individuals.

And the surface of the culture can be deceiving. Listening blithely to what people say can get you in trouble if you're not careful. The surface of the culture is typically thought of as the espoused values, better known as the values statement hanging on the wall and touted on the website. When you ask people about their organization's culture, they will inevitably show you a vision, mission, and values statement. All of these public statements are interesting because they tell us how the company wants to be perceived. No organization lives up to those statements perfectly. Some organizations come pretty close, and others routinely operate in ways that are diametrically opposed to the written values.

Enron is way up there on the top 10 list of corporate debacles of the twenty-first century. In a *New York Times* op-ed, James Kunen[3] wrote that the company website listed four values: respect, integrity, communication, and excellence. Those values are quite vague, fuzzy, and unfortunately, typical for the espoused values.

Here comes the interesting part. The Enron statement went on to say: "We do not tolerate abusive or disrespectful treatment. Ruthlessness, callousness, and arrogance don't belong here."

Wow. It is *not* typical to see the words *ruthlessness, callousness,* and *arrogance* in formal statements. Shakespeare's "the lady doth protest too much, methinks" comes to mind. Later cultural exploration after the company imploded clearly pointed to a culture of arrogance, ruthlessness, and callousness.

The real culture, or how things really work in a company with real, flawed leaders and employees, never plays out exactly as it sounds in the vision statement. Not to mention that there are many ways to interpret vague concepts like respect, integrity, communication, and excellence. Both leaders and followers must learn to decode and interact skillfully with culture in order to become more authentic. This chapter provides guidance on two key questions. First, what do you need to know about this thing called organizational culture in order to find the right fit for you? Second, what are the aspects of culture that matter most for you as a leader? Keep your self-knowledge in mind at all times as the alchemy between who you are and the culture is an element of what helps people grow or not grow as authentic leaders on a daily basis.

Whether you're a leader or a follower, decoding and interacting skillfully with various organizational cultures isn't easy. The most important thing you need to know about culture, though, is how to "read" it. We begin by getting into how to analyze your fit within any given culture. You'll need a high level of curiosity, a few ounces of skepticism, and basic knowledge from social science regarding the elements of organizational culture.

FIGURING OUT FIT

This thing we call organizational culture is a force of human nature. Many talented executives have failed to make change efforts work due to this powerful, multilayered force—so much so that you will often hear people say "that is just the culture" with an air of mystery in their voice as they passively accept negative behavior.

My pet peeve is to hear people say I need out of the "corporate" world as the culture is just awful. The social scientist in me is peeved because the corporate world is actually a pretty diverse place. Think of working at Zappos vs. working at Goldman Sachs. Both Zappos and Goldman Sachs are corporations and fall within the corporate world. Have you ever seen the CEO of Zappos in a suit? Take a minute and google Tony Hsieh, the CEO of Zappos, and look carefully at the images you see. On the other hand, have you ever seen the leadership of Goldman Sachs on television *not* in a custom suit? Just for a bit of contrast, google Lloyd Blankfein, the CEO of Goldman Sachs, and take in the visual. What differences do you notice between the two leaders? Working at Zappos as opposed to Goldman Sachs would be very different, and very few individuals would thrive in both places. Come to think of it, I can't come up with one individual who would thrive at both.

The Goldman Sachs vs. Zappos example is rather extreme. But even if you are an entry-level employee, do some research on the top company leaders before signing on. Leaders are the single most dominant force in shaping the culture. I am not saying that they are all-powerful, but top leaders have impact. I have had many senior-level clients in powerful positions who wish they had a magic culture transformation wand.

The variance in corporate cultures is something you need to comprehend and be a student of in order to continually put yourself in places that are a good fit. You also need to appreciate the diversity and complexity of culture in order to lead effectively. I always tell senior leaders to spend a solid 90 days trying to understand the culture just the way it is when they are entering an organization from the outside. This is not an easy sell, as executives are usually brought in to drive change, and they are chomping at the bit.

It is not as difficult to convince an executive who has already tried riding in from the outside and creating quick, massive change to hold off and go to school on the culture. We have frequent conversations about what they are learning. I have them asking for examples, getting people to tell them stories about former leaders, and studying the history of the place in detail. The reality is that organizational cultures vary a lot, even within the same industry and within the same organization. Working at Zappos would be different from working at Amazon, which actually owns

Zappos now. Furthermore, if you move from marketing to sales within the same organization, you may find totally different cultures. Beyond my peevishness when someone condemns the entire corporate world, I realize that the person has likely been having an awful experience within one particular corporation, with one particular boss or team. That human being has likely been operating in an overall corporate culture or within a team or divisional structure that is a terrible fit.

Think about a pair of shoes you bought that never fit right. Or imagine you are a size 10 and for some reason must wear a size 7. Maybe that size 7 is all you have with you. You can actually fall down and injure yourself in shoes that don't fit. Working in a place that is a bad fit for you is every bit as miserable as wearing a poorly fitting pair of shoes. Moreover, if your feet are hurting, you are not likely to be focused on the task at hand. Usually, a bad fit requires faking it to some degree, and you are not likely to be productive or authentic.

On the flip side of the coin, if you are working in an organization that is a good fit for you, just like a well-fitting pair of shoes, you will not even be aware of the culture. In a good cultural fit, you can focus, learn, and develop aspects of yourself as a leader and a follower.

Social science has much to offer in understanding this complex, powerful phenomenon called organizational culture. On a practical level, if you are in a culture that is not a fit with your values, you will struggle mightily. You are likely to be either miserable or unsuccessful, or both. None of us intentionally join a company or take a job that is a bad fit for us, but most of us have done it at least once.

How does that happen? It happens because we get in a hurry and also because the surface of a culture is often deceiving. How do we figure out fit and find a place to work that will support us in becoming more authentic or the best possible versions of ourselves? The point of view of an anthropologist is extremely helpful.

THE MIND-SET OF A CORPORATE ANTHROPOLOGIST

Adopting the mind-set of an anthropologist can help you find a fit in which you can grow as an authentic leader. You'll recall that anthropology is the study of people, past and present. Cultural anthropology is all about the study of cultures, focusing on how people live in particular places and how they organize, govern, and create meaning. Even brief study of cultural anthropology will leave you with an overwhelming sense of how much variety there is in the ways in which people can organize and form societies.

The tricky part is that the only people who can really "see" culture are outsiders—recall the analogy about the fish that can't describe the water it swims in. This is true in big and small ways. I grew up in the American South. When I have friends from the Northeast who venture south of the Mason-Dixon line, they always remark about how nice and friendly everyone is. I don't even notice it to this day. I just jump in gear as soon as I get off the plane, slow down, and start acting nicer. I don't have to think about it or wait on my relatives to reprimand me. I just do it automatically because I am a native of the South.

How does this relate to the business world? Once you have been in an organization or on a team for 30 days or so, you start taking certain things for granted. The novelty wears off. You become accustomed to the typical level of niceness and become acculturated. You become a part of the culture.

Anthropologists actually study cultures by going to live among societies and watching very closely. They take detailed field notes, especially early in the process. This observation of the culture while being in the culture is called ethnography or ethnographic research. Acting like an anthropologist and systematically observing our social groups is useful for both leaders and followers. The point at which the anthropologist becomes an insider is referred to as "going native."

When the anthropologist goes native, his or her ability to read the culture diminishes. Going native in the business world plays out like this as well. Let's say you join a new company. Within 30 days or so, you just start doing things the ways they are "supposed" to be done without a lot of conscious thought, especially if you are in a good fit for you. Dress is an obvious one. I was working with a client who was integrating into a new organization and he said "I need to go shopping pronto, Karissa." The new organization was extremely casual and he had a closet full of suits. Another easily observable one is how meetings are handled. In some organizations meetings start on time, period. In others, on time can mean 10 minutes after the appointed time. Pay attention to new people in your organization or think back to what seemed unusual when you were new. Chances are starting on time or 10 minutes late and the way you dress is taken for granted and you no longer have to think about it.

When I am serving as an advisor with the goal of helping to integrate a new executive into a new company, I encourage all of my clients to take their own version of field notes, especially during the first 30 days. Every day, they write what they noticed based on a useful, foundational model of organizational culture that we will get to in just a minute. The first step toward reading culture like an anthropologist is to get yourself a conceptual model or an organized way, grounded in social science, to think about businesses as cultures.

What exactly is a culture? All that is required to create a culture is for people to spend time together. When they do, norms or patterns of behavior are created. Very quickly, behaving outside the norm is not met with applause, but behaving within the norms is reinforced. These norms and approaches are heavily influenced by what helps the group meet its goals and what fails. The group does more of what works and less of what does not. Finally, the culture is heavily influenced by the leader's personality and way of thinking and doing. The culture can be heavily influenced by the leadership, whether the leader is a formal, identified leader or a leader who emerges.

Now that we've covered the basics of what cultures are and how they develop, you need a model for understanding one. As mentioned above, Edgar Schein created such a model based on the way anthropologists work. Schein says there are basically three levels of organizational culture. The first level is *artifacts*. Artifacts are physical symbols of a business. Any object that is easy to see is an artifact or a symbol of something in the organization.

Think of UPS. Both package delivery trucks and airplanes are artifacts. You have to be careful and notice the details of the artifacts, though, and ask questions if you are going to think like an anthropologist. On the surface, okay, there is a package delivery truck and an airplane and there are boxes. That makes good sense as they move boxes around the world using package delivery trucks and airplanes. That's it. But when you look more closely, what else do you observe? Why is the color brown used extensively? Have you ever seen a dirty UPS truck? Why or why not? If you asked about the cleanliness of the package car, you would discover that every truck is washed every day. If you have seen a dirty truck, you should call corporate headquarters in Atlanta because the leaders will likely be appalled. Why would UPS leaders be appalled in Atlanta about a dirty truck in Cleveland or China?

That brings us to Schein's second level of organizational culture, *espoused values*. UPS values the fact that every one of their vehicles looks the same, and that includes being clean. The espoused values, Schein's second level, are what the organization puts out on the website or frames on the wall.

Google "Procter & Gamble values" and you will see an example of espoused values. Procter & Gamble's values list in tidy straight lines integrity, leadership, ownership, passion for winning, and trust. Notice the font and the tone on the Procter & Gamble site. Procter & Gamble is and has been a leader in the consumer packaged goods industry for decades. Now, google "General Mills" and check out their values. You will see a big heart that says "we serve the world by making food people love." The values are called pursuits and are as follows: put people first, build a culture of creating, make food with passion, earn people's trust, and treat the world with care. Notice the emphasis on emotion in various ways on the General Mills site. Wow, what a contrast from Procter & Gamble—and both organizations are basically manufacturing household name brands like Cheerios and Bounty paper towels.

Would you rather work at General Mills or Procter and Gamble based on your Internet research and why? Take two minutes and write down your answer. Look at what you have written, and you could very well learn something about yourself that could be helpful in determining the kind of organization you need to be in to grow as an authentic leader. If you want to learn even more, have your spouse or a friend quickly go through the same exercise. Is their choice different from yours or the same? More important, what reasons influenced their choice?

Schein's first two levels are easy to see, but his third level is intriguing though difficult to see and read. If you as a leader have tried to make a change and it has been much harder than you expected, you are probably bumping up against the third level of organizational culture, *basic assumptions*. Basic assumptions are shared by all members of a group. Basic assumptions are not visible, they do not make any noise, and you will not find them on the values list. These basic assumptions take root in the organizational culture because they have driven success in the past. These basic assumptions are taken for granted and usually not even conscious.

Basic assumptions can often be traced all the way back to the beginning of the company and the perspective of the founder or early team. They only change when the company's survival is threatened, and even then, changing culture at the basic assumptions level is close to impossible. One of the basic assumptions in the American South is that it is better to be nice and friendly than brusque. The typical New Yorker living in Manhattan operates by a different set of basic assumptions about how to treat people. Basic assumptions are about how to treat people, the best ways to organize to get things done, or how to be successful. In some large manufacturing organizations, most of the senior leadership starts out working in an actual plant that makes whatever the company makes. The basic assumption at work there is that in order to understand the organization well enough to lead at the senior level, you need to have a solid working knowledge of the manufacturing process. In other manufacturing organizations, the vast majority of top leaders may come from marketing or sales. The basic assumption at work in those organizations is that people with deep customer knowledge will make better business decisions.

Let's go back to UPS. In 1996, I did my doctoral dissertation on the culture of UPS using the methods of anthropology and Schein's model. I interviewed individuals at various levels and functional groups while acting like an anthropologist and noting every detail.

There was much to learn about culture from UPS. I was totally intrigued as a doctoral student working in training at the UPS Airline in Louisville, Kentucky, when I noticed that no one took the water or coffee or whatever from the cafeteria back to their desk. There were no signs saying "no water or snacks outside the cafeteria." But if you had a coffee meeting, you had the meeting in the cafeteria and threw your cup out on the way. I started asking questions and people told me "that's just the way we do things." People were taken aback by the question at first. Then, we all got curious. I partnered with long-term insiders of the UPS culture and worked with them to understand the culture, which eventually turned into my dissertation. In case you are curious, the "no coffee at your desk" pattern of behavior was rooted in the notion that tidiness and orderliness leads to effectiveness. Tidiness and orderliness reigned throughout the whole building and are still obvious whenever I look at any UPS package truck.

If you want to understand an organization's current culture, you must go back to the beginning. What is the history of the company? This will always influence today's decisions in both obvious and covert ways, much the same way your history as an individual influences the choices you make today in ways you are aware of and in ways you take for granted.

UPS started out as a messenger and delivery service in 1907. The company was started in the Seattle area by a 19-year-old entrepreneur named Jim Casey. The competition was stiff, but Casey learned that if you provided the best service at low rates, you could win. According to the website, Casey's principle of best service, low rates still governs the company today.

If you have received or delivered a package, you know UPS has a big competitor called FedEx that also will deliver your packages anywhere in the world. Historically, one of the basic assumptions of the UPS culture was that the best decisions are made through data and quantitative analysis. And remember Jim Casey's adage "the best service at the lowest rate." There was a basic shared assumption in the culture that customers were price sensitive and looking to get their parcel to its destination as cheaply as possible. The company always used the most up-to-date analytical methods of looking at the business and potential strengths, weaknesses, opportunities, and threats through multiple analytical lenses. So one basic assumption—rooted all the way back to Jim Casey—was that low costs will help you be and stay successful, and decisions should be based on hardcore data and analysis. Those two things were basic assumptions and sound like common sense. In tandem, however, they kept UPS from moving rapidly into overnight deliveries in the 1980s.

The founder of FedEx, Fred Smith, started with a different set of assumptions in 1971. Smith noticed some industries like electronics and medicine had a need for overnight deliveries. From the beginning, FedEx was an airline designed to serve the market for urgent deliveries. UPS had been researching whether there was a market for such deliveries and, time and again, the research had indicated consumers would not pay for overnight and urgent deliveries, which would cost significantly more.

As you have probably figured out, Fred Smith was right and people— including you and me—are paying both FedEx and UPS for overnight deliveries on a routine basis, extra cost or not. So basic assumptions are both helpful and limiting.

Think of the organization you work in. What is taken for granted? This one isn't as easy to figure out. One clue is to notice what happens when two espoused values are in conflict. For example, Procter & Gamble's values list included both a passion for winning and integrity. What happens when winning and integrity are in conflict? How is the decision made? If you ask good questions, listen carefully, and watch what happens when values are competing or in conflict, you are likely to get to a basic assumption.

Kurt Lewin, a pioneer in organizational development, famously said if you want to understand a system, just try to change it. Seemingly logical changes that are not working are almost always in conflict with a basic assumption. For example, I have watched several client attempts to move the sales function to a tiered model. In a tiered model, different customers receive different levels of service based on how much money the company makes on their business. If one customer's business has a higher profit margin, that customer receives better service and priority treatment. That is a great idea in theory and will make a difference in the financials of any business. That is just common sense. That common sense neglects another fact. Many sales organizations and key individuals have been successful based on highly personal relationships with customers. The customer relationship can often evolve to be somewhat sacred. I have seen armies of sellers clap their hands at the new model and then be on the phone and strike a deal with a "special" customer the following Monday. That "special" customer is excused from the requirements of the new tiered system as a matter of course and the seller may or may not see the behavior as resistance to change. After all, that customer has stayed with that seller through thick and thin. In other words, salespeople have long-term relationships with customers, and customers are people, too. The closeness of those relationships often trumps the new initiative. Those sellers did not want their sacred relationship with that customer to be neglected regardless of whether or not the business was profitable or priority business. When you investigate such "resistance," you will almost always find a basic assumption like "take care of all your customers" that has proven to be a key to survival at some time in the organization's past.

So, now that you have a conceptual model and know that culture is not one thing but occurs at three levels, you can begin to notice artifacts and espoused values. You can also begin to be curious about the basic assumptions such as "cost is always a key driver."

Very few cultures are monolithic in this day and age. With globalization, and particularly in large companies like UPS or Procter & Gamble, you have many different cultures. Manufacturing will have a different culture than marketing, and so on. And all of the cultures will be influenced by the key leaders. Maintain your curiosity and take it all in with the mind-set of a corporate anthropologist. In the workouts, you will be using the new lens of corporate anthropologist to think about current and past experiences that were both positive and negative. The key is to learn from both good fits and bad fits. Many of my clients have actually learned the most about themselves through the terrible fits. Take the time to reflect and really take in the learning about yourself from all of your cultural encounters.

◈

THE WORKOUTS

- Imagine you just became CEO of your organization. How would you like to impact the culture, and what would you do in an effort to change the culture? How would your unique set of values translate into an organizational culture?

- Think of an environment that was a not a good fit for you. It may be your current one. Write about that environment for three minutes. What can you learn about yourself? What types of places should you avoid? How have you grown since that time, if it was in the past? Would it be a better fit now? Why or why not? If you are currently in a bad fit, what are the specific disconnects between the culture and who you really are?

- Think of an environment that was or is a good fit for you. Write about the environment for three minutes. Look at what you have written. What can you learn about yourself? Think like an anthropologist. What were the artifacts? What were the espoused values vs. the way things really worked? How did the conflicts between values get resolved? What happened? How was the place in sync with you? Not in sync with you? Remember there's no such thing as a "perfect" cultural fit. What can you learn about yourself from the positive experience? If the experience was in the past, how have you changed?

11

HOW TO MAKE PEACE WITH PARADOX

The fundamental state of leadership is not about being a wild card. It is not about being "authentic" in the sense of unloading our store of pent-up frustrations. It is about being purpose-centered, internally directed, other-focused, and externally open. "Letting the boss have it" is not the answer. Entering the fundamental state of leadership is much more demanding than that.

—Robert E. Quinn[1]

The simple answer (deceptively simple) is that to be a more effective leader, you must be yourself—more—with skill.

—Gareth Jones and Rob Goffee[2]

I checked my lipstick and looked directly in the mirror—painful enough given the harsh hotel bathroom lighting—to deliver my carefully crafted speech to my reflection: "Halle, I have a partner of

23 years who is a woman. I am gay. I know I should have told you at some point in the last 10 years, but I just could not find the courage." Actually, I only thought the last part, as a lump formed in my throat and the deepest part of my intestines clenched after I said the *I am gay* part out loud in the mirror.

I was getting ready for dinner with one of my favorite clients, who had become a friend over the years. We had worked together in multiple organizations on several large-scale executive development projects over the years. At that time, she was the head of talent development for Invesco, a large asset management company in Atlanta. Halle was savvy, quick witted, and could get more done in an afternoon than I could in a decade. Her bandwidth to coordinate projects that colleagues did not initially view as priorities, involving partnerships between multiple functions, was extraordinary. She was, in short, an executive whiz. As you might imagine, she had worked with various and sundry consultants of all varieties. Luckily for me, she found psychologists in particular to be an interesting lot. We developed a closer than normal alliance when—at the risk of getting fired—I told her something she really did not want to hear. Over the years, Halle had taken me in and always had sage advice about what I should do with my business, helping me understand that my differentiating strength is my ability to customize a psychological principle and apply it in a tailored way to a unique business situation. Her advice was invaluable, to the point where I would sometimes ask, "Are you sending me a bill this week or vice versa?"

Most recently, Halle had instructed me to get certified on the Hogan series of leadership assessment, despite my protests that I had completed enough psychological assessment training in graduate school to last a lifetime. Hogan Assessment Systems is a leading provider of quantitative personality assessments designed specifically for the practice of leadership. Hence, I was in Atlanta going to Hogan school, and one of my conditions was that Halle have dinner with me.

I was excited to see her, as she had won a battle with ovarian cancer and had been declared healthy almost a year before. We hadn't had real quality, in-depth time to talk live and in person since that wonderful news. We'd grown closer over the years as she had transitioned from one company to another and had struggled with the formidable challenge of managing the tough treatment necessary to combat ovarian cancer.

We'd had many conversations about what really makes a difference in life and work, spirituality, and meaning. While discussing the book *Autobiography of a Yogi*,[3] Halle laughed and said, "Karissa, you look like you are in the box and 'normal'—whatever that means—prancing around in those Armani jackets, but you are out there. You have a freak flag to fly that is all your own!" *Autobiography of a Yogi*, by the way, is certainly not a standard leadership development or business text, but it never fails to stretch the mind of anyone from the Western part of the world, especially a successful Western executive.

Don't worry. I am not suggesting that you need to read the classic story of the man who was one of the first to bring yoga to the Western world to stretch your mind and be authentic. However, I always challenge my clients to see and relate to the many paradoxes of personal and business leadership: Eastern approaches vs. Western approaches, theory and practice, short term and long term, the good of the team vs. the individual, and so on.

Right before our dinner that night, I was wrestling with a personal paradox myself. The gulf between the depth of our relationship and the fact that I had not shared a very basic part of who I was—yet another freak flag—with Halle was eating at me. It just did not feel right. I had several bullet points to defend my lack of self-disclosure such as irrelevance, we live in different cities, and I am in a professional role. And my best and finest bullet point: She is so smart, she has this figured out. The great thing about the last bullet was that it applied to all my clients! Despite those fine bullet points, I felt fake and inauthentic because I could not find the courage to be truthful about my life. Hence the rehearsal in front of the mirror. As you have probably already figured out, I am a cautious soul as opposed to an open book.

I slid into our assigned table at a fashionable sushi joint in midtown. Halle arrived and I was taken aback by how fabulous and healthy she looked. We settled in, ordered drinks, and just I was taking a deep breath and getting ready to out with it literally, she looked me straight in the eye and said, "I am really glad we are having dinner tonight. I got the news today that my cancer is back, and the prognosis is not good."

My gut tightened, and a deep sorrow literally brought tears to my eyes and hers. I said absolutely nothing. I sat there for a few minutes, processing what I thought Halle might be feeling along with the emotional tide that was coursing through. She broke the silence by saying, "I was relieved to be having dinner with you because I knew that you would not try to fix this or put a positive spin on it. That we could just be with the reality and that I would not have to put on a brave face." Halle continued with authenticity, "I don't feel good about it and I am not grateful yet." She expressed her anger and sadness full-throttle. Several minutes later, she added, "But I do feel grateful to have had the last year as a healthy person."

I smiled at that comment, as one of her strengths that I appreciated was her seemingly indefatigable optimism through cancer, career crises, and basically anything. Her strengths of optimism and gratitude were starting to blossom in the space. We relaxed into the conversation and I was her confidante as we cried and laughed and talked about what the prospect of dying in the shorter term meant to her. What did she think was important? She was most sorry to be leaving her husband of over two decades alone early.

That was the last time I saw Halle, as she took leave from work, spent quality time with her family, and passed away 18 months after that dinner. My hotel room rehearsal was wasted energy, as my gayness seemed inconsequential in the context of our conversation that evening.

That evening became a wake-up call for me on several levels. Halle's comment—that she trusted she could share the terrible news with me and I wouldn't try to "fix it" or make her feel as though she had to put on a brave face for my benefit—was a recognition of one of my deepest gifts. In allowing people to be who they are and feel exactly what they feel, my clients grow and become bigger, grander versions of themselves right in front of my eyes.

How was it that I struggled to be authentic in the very act of creating space for others to be whomever they needed to be?

Here comes the paradox, or the apparent contradiction. I am someone who is brave enough to be with people as they face their own mortality, but too chicken to say out loud that I am gay. Something about that whole paradox struck me as a "developmental gap," as we coaches like to say, or maybe I had outgrown the fear that had defined a much earlier part of my life, especially with people I really valued.

You have paradoxes of your own if you dig deep enough and really start working at authenticity in a meaningful way. We are all a paradox. We humans are a mixture of courage and cowardice, brilliance and buffoonery, and morality and hypocrisy. There is no way to be authentic as a leader without understanding and effectively making peace with the paradox that is you, the paradox that is other people, and the paradox that is rampant in making business decisions in the twenty-first century. The title of this chapter, "How to Make Peace with Paradox," is a playful nod to the realities of negotiating with real-life situations and finding ways to be true to yourself, paradoxes and all, more times than not.

Paradoxes aren't ever "solved," but managed and negotiated over and over. Making peace with paradox is about the fact that you and I will need to manage our personal paradoxes in different ways at different phases of our lives and careers.

Why Should Anyone Be Led By You? is the title of a thoughtful book on authentic leadership by Gareth Jones and Rob Goffee and also a damn good question. Take a minute and let that one sink in. If you can get past feeling threatened, the question is powerful. Many recurrent human dilemmas are underneath those seven words. Should people follow you because you are similar to them or because you are different? What is so special and unique about you? What are the strengths that set you apart? How do you use your strengths? What are your weaknesses that you should hide? Or should you hide your weaknesses? Many of us have been told to hide our weaknesses at various times in our lives. And our uniqueness has not always been met with applause from the herd. Our differences may have been met with outright rejection and harshness.

The words of Jones and Goffee instruct us to be ourselves, but not too much. Don't offend. Don't rock the boat. "Being yourself" turns into a complicated thing by the time we are teenagers and start processing all those messages. We internalize a mixture of messages and have certain patterns of behavior that become routinized and, in many cases, unexamined. We know what works and what doesn't—we think.

This chapter will challenge your view of what works in a quest for what might work even better. We will look at not just what works or is average but what is amazing. We will use the lens of positive psychology and positive organizational scholarship to deepen your journey toward being more authentic.

Your power and presence as an authentic leader come from who you are, paradoxically including strengths and weaknesses and similarities and differences from other people. Your uniqueness is in the mix of towering strengths and outrageous flaws and the ways you are like others and the ways you are different from your reference groups. Learning to deploy that unique blend that is you, to make extraordinary things happen in business and your life, is the central challenge of authentic leadership. This chapter delves into the realities of deploying who you are at a deep level to the task of leadership.

Who Are You (Really)?

Becoming a more authentic leader requires that we challenge ourselves to go deeper than personality, competencies, and goals. We must wrestle with those paradoxes that are a part of the complicated system of you. Who you are and where you come from at a fundamental level really matter. In the words of the classic English rock band the Who, "Who are you"? We psychologists use the word *identity* to capture the notion of who you are at a fundamental level. Being willing to grapple with identity by dealing with tough, threatening questions takes practice and commitment. But maintaining an accurate concept of who you are on an internal level and what signals you send to others is a must if you want to become a more authentic leader.

Let me give you an example of what I mean by "grappling." As an executive coach, I am often asked to meet potential clients either live or on the phone. It is essentially a job interview for me. The typical executive meets with two or three coaches and chooses the coach he or she feels most comfortable with in many executive development programs. These meetings often feel like beauty contests for the coach, but I make a concerted effort to really give the client a sense of what it is like to work with me as a coach, as opposed to sounding like an advertisement or telling a client what I think they want to hear.

I once had two beauty pageant interviews with executives in two different organizations on the same day. Ironically, both executives had been asked to work on the fact that their team, peers, and boss perceived them to be arrogant. Both were super smart and had unique skills in particular technical domains. The first potential client explained that he had just gotten feedback that he was perceived to be arrogant, and had been asked to work with a coach. His first few questions were centered on how exactly this coaching thing works. We went into all that. Then, he asked me if I had questions for him. My question for him was, "Are you arrogant?" This was not a good choice to make a good impression in a beauty contest! He paused for what seemed like a long time. And he said, "I don't know. If you would have asked me that six months ago, I would have said yes, but I am really over my head technically right now for the first time in my life."

We delved into that a bit on the phone and a lot during the next year. He selected me and I was excited to work with him. He was not in his comfort zone dealing with the "are you arrogant?" question, but he somehow knew it was an important question if he was going to really grow as a leader.

Moving on to the second beauty contest interview of the day, the first half of the conversation moved along with niceties. I explained how coaching generally works again. Then, the client said "the key issue is that I am perceived to be arrogant." Remember my notion that authentic leaders must be willing to really grapple with tough questions of identity in an ongoing manner.

You know what's coming. "Are you arrogant?" I asked.

No pause. "There is no way anyone could work in this place without being confident," he declared dismissively. "I've been promoted three times in five years. The issue is not whether I am arrogant. The issue to be addressed is the perception." He went on to put me in my place in multiple ways within the next 10 minutes.

This was not a battle that I was choosing to fight. I moved us on to another issue as quickly as I possibly could and ended the call with some final niceties. As you probably have guessed, he did not pick me to be his coach. The first guy was willing to grapple with fundamental questions of identity and at least on that particular day, the second guy was not willing to go there. Issues of identity are not part of most everyday conversations and they are threatening by their very nature. Very few people will look in the mirror in the morning and think "I am arrogant and people don't really like me" with pride!

We all like to keep a stable, clear idea of who we are that is generally positive. But in periods of growth that involve moving out of our comfort zone, we have to be willing to examine and reexamine issues of identity. We have to be willing to look at deep value conflicts and sides of our character and personality that are not virtuous, effective, or pleasant. In the process of grappling, you are also likely to also become more aware of signature strengths and gifts that you may not fully acknowledge, either. Becoming more authentic is not possible if you aren't willing to move outside your comfort zone and do the grappling work. Grappling is a process of self-discovery and investigation that is ultimately gratifying, if not always fun.

⟨✷⟩

THREE SELVES THAT WON'T MAGICALLY ALIGN

One of the ways in which I stir my clients to grapple with key identity issues is through the introduction of three concepts: the ideal self, the real self, and the ought self. All three concepts have a rich history in psychology, but they were first articulated together by E. Tory Higgins[4] and referred to as *self-discrepancy theory*. (Remember, central to being authentic in practical terms is this idea of multiple selves and selves awareness that was discussed at length in Chapter 5.)

The ongoing articulation and understanding of all three of the selves described by Higgins is a useful practice for authentic leaders. However, the most important of the three for authentic leadership development is the ideal self. The ideal self is who you want to be. It is you at your best and is essentially a personal vision of who you desire to be. The ideal self is usually less conscious than the real self. Your real self is who you perceive yourself to be, just like it sounds. We all carry around in our heads a perception of ourselves that we can usually articulate quickly. I ask my clients questions such as "who were you in that situation?" or "what role did you play in creating that particular outcome?" Answers to such questions usually come pretty quickly and usually generate constructive dialogue.

The ideal self is more complex, and generally less top of mind than the real self. However, the clear articulation of the ideal self in a form that is meaningful for you as an individual is powerful. It sets in motion a desire to be more like your ideal self as well as a flood of positive emotions, including hope, optimism, and physiological energy.[5] The articulation of the ideal self is an intellectual and emotional exercise. By articulating a vision of your ideal self, you are also figuring out what has personal meaning for you as a unique human being and leader. Prompts such as "tell me a story of you at your best" or "tell me something that you accomplished that you are really proud of" tend to ensure we are getting at both emotion and uniquely personal meaning, and not just doing some intellectual exercise as we are using the ideal self as a conceptual tool. Ultimately, most of my clients have an ideal self-proclamation that is unique to them. Some are bullet points. Others are paragraphs.

Let's do an experiment. Stop for three minutes and just write down what comes to mind when you think about you at your best. This process is worth a bigger investment of time, but jotting down your first thoughts is a great place to start. What themes do you notice? What really matters is that the output is personally meaningful to you.

The third self, the ought self, is a great tool to use when you are feeling pressured to compromise. The ought self is just like it sounds: who you ought to be according to other people, including authority figures. Clearly drawing the contrast between your ideal self (who *you* think you should be) vs. the ought self (who *others* think you should be) in specific, pressure-filled situations can be extremely helpful.

Let me offer an example from reality. One of my clients had articulated a desire to have more balance in her life. She was a service-oriented person and had a hard time saying no. Part of her ideal self-proclamation was that she honored all the commitments in life, including her commitment to family. She had planned a vacation with her family and casually mentioned to me during our update that she was canceling the trip because an important project was running behind schedule.

I started investigating and found out her boss had looked relieved when she told him she was thinking about canceling her vacation. I asked my client several more questions, and we discovered together that her ought self had taken over, and she had lost track of her ideal self after that conversation with her boss. It became clear to both of us that her ought self had kicked into high gear and drove the decision to cancel her vacation. I, of course, asked her how this decision jived with honoring commitments to *all* the people in her life, which was part of her ideal self.

We both agreed that her real self really wanted and needed a vacation. The clarification of all three selves was not a panacea. However, the conversation did open the door for her to reconsider the decision to cancel the vacation and raise her awareness regarding the tensions between her ideal self, ought self, and real self. She wound up shortening the trip but still going, which allowed her to feel that she was honoring *all* of her commitments.

Using the conceptual tools of the ideal self, the real self, and the ought self is a valuable practice for both personal and leadership development. Next, we will turn our attention to the notion of leadership itself. We will focus on managing the unique set of paradoxes that is you on a daily basis. You can be an authentic leader in one moment and not so authentic in the next. (Me, too.)

◈

AUTHENTIC LEADERSHIP IS A STATE OF MIND

What is your state of mind right now? Is your monkey mind in charge and are you thinking about your grocery list while skimming this book? How about your mood? Irritable? Fussy? Relaxed? Our states of mind and heart vary and can change rapidly. The notion of cultivating a state of mind that is productive, or a winner's mind-set, is often discussed and accepted as a key to success in our culture. However, we tend to think most often of leadership as an assigned role or title, or we gravitate toward lofty, rather complicated, highly varied and often confusing definitions of leadership.

For example, Brittney Helmrich,[6] a writer and editor at *Business News Daily*, asked 30 entrepreneurs for their definition of leadership and titled her article "Thirty Definitions of Leadership." From her interviews, she came up with 30 rather lofty, somewhat abstract definitions. If you are at work, you could likely walk down the hall and talk to 10 people and write a similar article.

Not much is discussed as often and understood as little as leadership. I cajole most of my clients into coming up with a definition that makes sense to them, even if they steal it from Warren Bennis or Peter Drucker or *Business News Daily*. The litmus test is whether my clients can give me an example or anecdote of how the definition relates to their personal leadership. If there is no example, my radar for being worked starts going off and they get a look. *Being worked*, simply put, is when my clients are just saying something to get me off their back. You know what I mean. We have all done it. There is no real thought or heartfelt meaning behind what is being said.

Robert E. Quinn, a professor at the University of Michigan and a leader in the emerging field of positive organizational scholarship, offered up a pragmatic twist on all of the leadership pontificating. Quinn described leadership as a fundamental state of mind, and you are a leader when you enter what he terms the fundamental state of leadership. This hit home for me on a practical level, as I have noted over the years how hard it is for executives to process how they behave as leaders while in the midst of 500 e-mails, the crisis du jour, and/or dealing with two or three bosses in a matrix organization.

All of my clients write a one-page leadership development plan. We have updates twice a month. It is not uncommon for them to say how nice it is during our updates to step back and actually think about what they have been experiencing from the point of view of who they are as leaders, and who they want to be as leaders. Often, I watch as my clients enter a leadership state of mind and begin to make connections they have not been making in the midst of the daily grind.

From my own point of view, authentic leadership in particular is best described as a fundamental psychological state. Just like any psychological state or state of mind, you can't stay in it all the time. But with practice, you can cultivate the fundamental state of authentic leadership and be in that state of mind more often. As Quinn points out, this notion of leadership as a fundamental state makes more sense in contrast to the normal human state. Quinn describes the "normal" state as:

- self-focused
- externally directed
- comfort-centered
- internally closed

In contrast to the "normal state," Quinn describes the fundamental state of leadership as:

- other-focused
- internally directed
- purpose centered
- externally open

Self-focused is quite familiar to most of us, meaning we are out to meet our own personal goals and put our own interests first. When we enter the state of leadership, however, we shift and become other-focused. Practically speaking, we do not forget our own agenda, but we do put the overarching goal of the team or business first and are as aware of others as we are of ourselves.

Paradoxically, helping my clients become more other-focused with questions typically lifts their moods. In other words, they become livelier and more positive when they focus on others rather than themselves. Often, in those coaching updates, I witness my clients shifting and beginning to take on the perspectives of other key players in the organization, including their boss, direct reports, and peers. It takes prompting and reprogramming the mind-set regularly, but we can all be more other-focused.

In a normal state, we humans tend to be externally directed, meaning we are thinking about how we are perceived and working hard at getting resources, often in a win-or-lose way. For example, when you are constantly trying to impress your boss to get a bigger budget, you are externally directed. You are not likely to forget which person is your boss or lose awareness of the resources you need. However, when you enter what Quinn terms the state of leadership, you become more internally directed and monitor your own leadership behaviors. You ask yourself those tough questions, such as "am I behaving as my ideal self or am I behaving arrogantly?" When you are in an internally directed state, you grapple and deal with lack of alignment between your ideal self and your real self in a straightforward manner and habitually take steps to live more in alignment with your ideal self. You can also experience the positive emotions associated with living in alignment with your own values when you are internally focused.

The third component of Quinn's state of leadership is being purpose centered as opposed to comfort centered. The normal, comfort-centered state is reactive to the environment and strives for protection. We try to avoid pain and get pleasure. In contrast, the purpose-centered state is about your overarching goal or purpose. Being purpose centered allows you to get out of your comfort zone and into a growth zone because you are not thinking about your comfort, you are thinking about a bold, audacious goal instead.

The fourth component, being internally closed, means you are executing what you know will work and missing subtle cues that you might need to adapt or change it up. In the state of leadership, or what I am adapting to say the state of authentic leadership, you are externally open, noticing what is working, and paying attention to all cues. You are continually adapting what you are doing at least in small ways, and have your radar attuned enough to pick up on necessary changes.

Let's take this from the textbook to reality. I worked with a newly formed team that was a mix of people from two newly merged companies. Like most merged companies, the companies had vastly different policies and cultures. Everything you learned in Chapter 10 about organizations as cultures applies to this situation.

The leader of the team was from company A. The rest of the team was about half company A and half company B. In general, those cultural differences melted away as the whole team entered a state of authentic leadership on most days and were highly purpose centered. They were working on an intense project to integrate two information technology systems in a period of six months. They had countdown-to-going-live posters all over the place, and the team spirit was contagious. The pressure to perform and visibility were high. As a result, they were spending more time with each other than their families and becoming very cohesive.

Tragedy struck one of the team members when both of his parents were killed in an automotive accident. The leader from company A called the team together to let them know what had happened, and that he would be sending flowers from the team and traveling to go to the funeral. After the meeting, one of the team members from company B said, "You know the company won't cover your travel or the flowers. That is just not our policy." In the merge, all of the human resource policies of company B replaced those of company A.

When confronted with this fact, the leader of the team (from company A, who'd always kept budgets for flowers and such when tragedy struck employees) got red in the face and entered the normal human state and became internally closed, self-focused, externally directed, and comfort centered in the span of two minutes. He quipped a few curse words and declared, "I will just do it myself." The other team member from company B was shocked, as he had never seen the boss lose his cool.

Meanwhile, the greenest, youngest, lowest-paid member of the team had been following along behind and listening to the conversation. That team member said, "Let's all chip in for a gift, and some of us should take off and make it a road trip to go to the funeral."

The other two took a minute to process what he said and were jolted into a state of leadership. All three became other focused (focusing on what would be most helpful for the team member who had lost both his parents) and purpose centered (being there for their colleague has value and meaning). To the boss's credit, he also used the incident to be externally open and internally directed as he recounted his personal learning about how to relate to this new culture as well as his learning about himself during our next update call. He said he had learned that he could be rigid at times. He shared this lesson with his wife, who agreed wholeheartedly and laughed at his newfound self-knowledge. In the realm of being externally open and continually learning, his view was that every team member chipping in and half the team making the road trip had meant more to the bereaved employee than him making the trip and the company paying for the gift could have possibly meant.

Much to your likely relief, I rarely offer my clients the whole conceptual model that we just went through! However, I have found four questions that can shift my client's mind-set toward a state of authentic leadership. Any one of these four can take us into productive developmental conversations way below the surface of things. Play with one or more of the questions below on a regular basis and notice what happens to your mind-set.

The deceptively simple questions are:

1. What is the perspective of your boss, colleague, or peer? (other-focused)

2. How is this behavioral choice in alignment or not with your values? (internally directed)

3. Shift up a few thousand feet. What is the overarching goal? (purpose centered)

4. What have you learned in the last few weeks? (externally open)

The vast majority of us spend some portion of our time in a state of authentic leadership in which we are other focused, internally directed, purpose centered, and externally open. The goal is to increase the amount of time we spend in the state of authentic leadership and not rely on our environment to move us in that direction.

⌘

THE WORKOUTS

- Identify a trusted friend or colleague and ask them to complete a 30-minute exercise with you. The first step is to think about a time when you were at your most authentic. Tell the story to your trusted friend or colleague. Then, have your trusted friend or partner do the same thing. Discuss the similarities and differences between the two stories.

- I use a simple exercise to make the concept of the ideal self tangible for my clients. Give it a try. Imagine you have accomplished your goals as a leader and are being true to yourself at the same time. What do you see? I ask them to respond to the prompt on at least three separate days and write for a minimum of 15 minutes. They have to keep writing for 15 minutes, no matter what and no editing. Take the output and highlight the themes. You are on your way to creating an ideal self-proclamation.

- One of the paradoxes identified by Jones and Goffee is a recurrent challenge for a lot of my clients. The paradox is "be close and be far," meaning be approachable but also keep an appropriate distance that allows you to make authoritative decisions when necessary. How do you navigate that one? Do you tend to be too distant or too close? What could you do that would help you make peace with that particular paradox?

12

How to Ferociously Seek the Truth (When Everyone Is Framing and Spinning)

When well-being comes from engaging our strengths and virtues, our lives are imbued with authenticity.
　　　　　—Martin Seligman's Twitter Self-Description[1]

Authenticity is knowing, and acting on, what is true and real inside yourself, your team, and your organization AND knowing and acting on what is true and real in the world. It is not enough to walk one's talk if one is headed off, or leading one's organization, community, or nation off, a cliff.

　　　　　　　　　　　　　　　　　—Robert Terry[2]

Leadership is all about two words now. It is about truth and trust.
Let's say you are the boss and have a conference room down the hall.
People are coming in and spinning you. You have to look out for your
people when they hit it out of the park and when they don't. Then, they
trust you. When they trust you, you get the truth. When you get the
truth, you get speed. Then, you can act.

—Jack Welch[3]

I was finishing up my day and thinking about pizza for dinner when an e-mail popped up from a client named Ken. All the e-mail said was CALL ME in all caps on the subject line. This couldn't be good. I sighed and dialed the number. Live from Brussels, Ken yelled into my ear: "Every single member of my staff has been lying to me! For months!"

I lowered the volume on my speakerphone. It was 4 PM for me on the East Coast of the United States and 9 PM for him in Brussels. In his booming baritone, Ken continued: "Why on earth am I finding out *now* that Project Turn Key is six weeks behind and needs 2 million more to have a chance of finishing by the end of the year?"

It was Halloween, October 31. Ken had just been informed of this development via e-mail. The project team had sent him a joint e-mail making the request for more money and time at 3:45 PM EST, no doubt hoping the boss would sleep on it before responding. Reading between the lines, and given that he was in Brussels, they may have also hoped he'd had a few drinks with dinner.

Years ago, I had been Ken's coach and we had worked on his tendency to be reactive and go off when he heard bad news. Now, we just talked periodically, and I served as his advisor. Ken was responsible for implementing momentous changes as his organization coped with a recession and market conditions that were more like a hurricane than headwinds.

After quite a bit of empathic listening on my part, we began to devise a strategy for Ken to respond in a way that would make it more likely instead of less likely that he would know sooner next time. These "hot moments," when your emotions are running high and you feel as if you've been lied to, are critical, as they are ripe for learning how to become more honest and authentic for leaders and team members alike. Leaders need to be careful not to reinforce less-than-desired behavior—such as e-mailing very bad news across the Atlantic at the last minute—by stirring up fear and punishing people. To be clear, the leader must address the less-than-desired behavior. However, addressing that behavior in a hot state is not likely to be productive.

Ken and I decided he would not respond by phone or e-mail at all while in Brussels. Instead, he would call a live meeting with the team and embody the courage it takes to deal with inconvenient truths face-to-face and eye-to-eye, on the same continent in the same room. At some point, he might ask his team to not blindside him with an e-mail. However, allowing them to stew for a few days and then look the boss in the eye was much more likely to land the lesson than a tirade of any kind. And there would be a next time for bad news, no matter what.

This is the reality of running a business involving contractors, technical experts, big stakes, moving parts with different interests, and lots of money. The story is relevant whether you are an entrepreneur running a small business or a leader in a large global organization. Stuff always happens and things never go exactly as planned.

At least once a week, one of my senior-level clients will complain to me that no one is telling them the truth. What does this mean? Why don't people just tell the truth? Are thousands of hardworking people intentionally lying and morally bankrupt? Some people are. But it is far from typical. So if they're not all bad seeds, what is really going on with my clients, and perhaps where you work as well?

❦

THE TRUTH SERUM QUESTION

Many individuals in leadership roles at all kinds of companies complain to me that getting to the truth about what is going on in a business situation can be elusive. If they are in a calm, rational state while complaining, I often ask them my "truth serum" question as we sort through their frustration. This is a tool for realistically understanding the issues that keep you and others (leaders and followers) from simply telling the truth.

Here is the truth serum question: What would happen in your workplace tomorrow if everyone took a very powerful truth serum and said exactly what they thought every minute of the day? No filters, no framing, and no spinning. Imagine if everyone said exactly what they thought about the new project to cut costs on supply chain, your behavior, how they wished they could go home, or mused about how their new pants looked or that you were looking fat. Take two or three minutes and imagine that one. What might your boss do or say? What about the members of your team? Your closest associates? Your romantic partner or family members? What would you be saying or doing under the influence of the truth serum? Aside from the irrelevant, random thoughts, what substantive views or concerns are you holding back on? The vast majority of those same clients who are frustrated with getting the truth out of others are also holding back on something themselves.

After the initial chuckle in response to the truth serum question, clients almost universally add: "Maybe we could get something done for a change." As Jack Welch says in the epigraph, they perceive that people are coming in every day and spinning them. And my clients are usually right. People *are* coming in everyday and spinning them. Without skillful, authentic leadership that ferociously seeks the truth, the spinning will continue. You must skillfully seek the truth and understand the forces that keep people from telling you the truth.

After we get the initial responses to the truth serum question out of the way, the conversation goes in some interesting directions. Clients typically react first to the no-filter idea. Most of my senior-level clients will say something like, "I filter myself not because I want to lie, but because I've learned that my first reaction to most things is not in sync with the way I might think or feel an hour later. Those unfiltered first reactions can do a lot of harm."

We can all relate to that one. Most of us can recall a time when we quickly reacted to something and regretted it within an hour or the next day. E-mail can be dastardly in this way, as it allows us to react quickly and leaves a permanent record. Many careers and relationships have been irreparably damaged by an e-mail that was "truthful in the moment" when it was sent. Of course, many of the judgments that float through our minds about someone gaining weight or looking good in new pants are totally irrelevant and potentially harmful. However, knowing what is and is not relevant regarding complex business issues is not as simple as it sounds for leaders or team members. What comes around goes around. When I talk with team members, they are also often frustrated because they feel their boss forgets to tell them information that could save them time. Then we talk about the practical need at times to put a positive spin on things, not just for the team or organization, but for yourself. Those truth serum conversations become quite interesting and layered.

Where can authentic leaders draw the line without magic truth serum or black-and-white formulas? Is it possible to acknowledge an ugly or inconvenient truth and still see potential in the midst of bad news? Sometimes it is, and sometimes it is not. Leading authentically and ferociously seeking the truth are full of this kind of subtlety, nuance, and the frustrating absence of black-and-white. To be sure, we have all witnessed revolting breaches of ethics that were clearly black. But for the most part, day-to-day realities in business are much more subtle and complicated than felonies.

Back to Ken and Project Turn Key. When exactly did the project team know for sure that they were going to need more money in order to finish by the end of the year? Were they overly optimistic, or were they each focusing on their own silo and losing sight of the whole? As you might have guessed, further investigation of the situation did not yield a conspiracy to make Ken have a heart attack in Brussels! Further investigation did reveal a web of misunderstanding and, paradoxically, decision making that had been made too fast and without fully exploring potential implications and unintended consequences.

To be sure, framing and spinning can be used to hide from reality and avoid inconvenient truths. On the other hand, framing up challenges in a way that is empowering to the team instead of defeatist or pessimistic actually influences reality or the truth of our daily situation. Conversations with clients after the truth serum query point out the inherent complexities of seeking truth over speaking pure facts.

First and foremost, the human brain naturally interprets events and finds relationships between events. We are constantly telling ourselves stories about what is happening around us. This constant interpretation and storytelling in our own heads is so ingrained that it takes effort for us to be aware of the stories we are telling ourselves. Hence, the truth about any situation is usually not one single fact but often a matter of interpretation involving many perspectives—and that applies even in everyday, simple dilemmas like who is supposed to unload the dishwasher tonight, never mind a complex initiative involving hundreds of people collaborating to achieve a tough goal in a compressed amount of time.

Authentic leaders are committed to actively seeking the truth with an awareness that the truth in many real-life and work situations is not permanent, straightforward, or simple. Regardless of your current role, understanding the dynamics of telling the truth—or not—is useful. If you are in an earlier stage of your career, you don't necessarily want to just emulate what you see around you without thinking. People in your work environment may be playing it overly safe. People are likely emotionally defensive, scared, and playing it safe, but as we learned in Chapter 10, organizational cultures vary a lot. People may be reckless with facts and other people's feelings in your work environment. As Robert Terry's epigraph indicates, leading a team off a cliff in the pursuit of authenticity and truth accomplishes nothing. Regardless of the culture, find your own way to be who you are with full awareness and respect for the overall culture. Think for yourself and figure out how you can seek the truth and have a positive impact on the business situation and the people around you.

This last chapter is about the pursuit of truth. As we all know, we tend to end speeches, meetings, articles, and books with ideas that really matter and should be prioritized over other ideas when you have to choose, and this closing chapter is no exception. Nothing matters more in the process of becoming a more authentic leader and human being than the ferocious pursuit of truth.

All of us naturally link the notion of authenticity with seeking and telling the truth instinctively, and scholars in psychology and philosophy do the same. In this chapter, we will use the science of psychology to shed light on practical situations, such as why my client was not warned that Project Turn Key was behind. We will also bring relevant insights from positive psychology and positive organizational scholar-ship to the task of attending to the deeper, more complex dimensions of truly becoming a more authentic leader. How do you craft who you are and your character so that you are a leader who seeks and speaks the truth and helps others do the same? Intentionally cultivating the deeper, more virtuous aspects of your character sets up conditions where you are more likely to get the truth from key direct reports, peers, and even your boss.

First, let's look at the practical dynamics that cause people to "spin," as Jack Welch termed it in the epigraph, as opposed to telling leaders the truth.

THE TRUST METER IS ALWAYS RUNNING

Here is the practical reality about leading, truth, and trust. If you are the leader, you must prove you are trustworthy. The burden of proof is on you, the leader. You are assumed dangerous until proven otherwise. And you are being observed and tested every day and moving up or down on the trustworthiness meter of every individual on your team. The general factors that compose workplace trust are judgments of integrity, ability, and benevolence. Integrity is about whether you as the leader are being honest or dishonest. Ability is about whether your people perceive you to be competent in your particular technical area and as a leader. Benevolence is about whether you as a leader really care about your people or whether you see them as essentially resources like money or computers.[4]

You don't get an automatic pass on integrity, ability, or benevolence. If you want your followers to trust you, you have to prove yourself over and over. Unfortunately, it only takes one action or behavior—partic-ularly in a high-pressure situation—to cancel out months of perceived trustworthiness. If you are currently leading a team, arm yourself right now with the insight that the trust meter is always running, and don't forget it.

You must look out for your people when things are going well for them and when they are struggling to produce desired results. The way you choose to react and respond when people make mistakes or fall short on goals always matters, so choose carefully.

I know what you are thinking: "Of course I am trustworthy. I have never done anything to person X to prove otherwise." That's just it. You have to realize it is human nature to play it safe. Decades of research in social psychology and common sense have proven over and over again that it is human nature to play it safe if you are a lower-status person interacting with a higher-status person. Everyone has a boss unless you are the chairman of the board and CEO in a public company. (Many people in the position of chairman and CEO would tell you that they would rather have one identifiable boss, but you get my point.) Think of how you behave with your boss as opposed to your direct reports or peers. Unless you have a highly unusual relationship, you are more careful and more guarded when you interact with your boss as well as other people in the organization who rank higher than you. People who are higher ranking have the power to hurt those of lower rank, and that is just the way it is. As noted in Chapter 10, we humans are still tribal in many ways.

It is up to you as the leader to create conditions in which people feel safe enough to tell the truth. If you can learn how to create those conditions, your chances of being furious and learning bad news late in the game go down exponentially. That is not to say you will not have isolated incidents in which individuals on your team lie to you, even if you work to create the right conditions. Dealing with that stuff is part of being a leader and you may have to step up and remove individuals from your team if they just can't live up to telling the truth. Most work occurs in teams now, so this process of shaping norms of behavior is even more powerful than it would have been 20 years ago. Your job as the leader is to behave in a way that creates norms involving telling the truth and facing reality. How do you create those norms?

On a specific level, you as the leader must embody the behaviors you wish to see in your team. Let's go back to Ken in Brussels and the Project Turn Key debacle for a moment. When I asked Ken what he wished had happened instead, he said he wished the team would have called a live meeting with him and told him this news face-to-face. Therefore, we decided he would call a live face-to-face meeting to discuss the situation. One could argue it was mean of Ken to not respond right away, as he knew the team would be stewing. We decided it was more important for him to embody the desired behavior. Ken and I also made use of the research conducted by Amy Edmondson[5] of Harvard Business School on ways to cultivate psychological safety as we carefully navigated this learning moment with the Project Turn Key team. The following factors from Edmondson's work were relevant to Ken's situation and are relevant in general for creating psychological safety in teams:

- Be accessible and approachable.
- Display your own fallibility.
- Highlight failures as learning opportunities.
- Hold people accountable for transgressions.
- Clarify boundaries and expectations.

Being accessible and approachable sounds easy enough until you look at the actual number of meetings on most of my clients' calendars. If you are in any kind of professional position in a modern organization, the demands on your time are extreme. The process of ruthless prioritization comes into play here. If you as a leader want to cultivate psychological safety, you have to make time to spend with your people either on the phone or in person. You must respond to e-mails quickly or set an expectation that you will respond within a specific period of time.

There is no substitute for putting in the time to build the relationships. Jane Dutton (2003)[6] of the University of Michigan has articulated the value of what she terms "high-quality connections." Central to the idea of high-quality connections is being really present when you spend time with your team as a group or as individuals. This means no iPhone swiping, e-mailing, texting, or taking phone calls in meetings with your people. Many clients of mine have transformed their relationships with teams and individuals by simply putting away all distractions during the time they have to be with people both on the phone and in person. If you can't get rid of some meetings and make more time, you can make the time you do have of a higher quality. Doing both is a good idea. A lot of my clients grimace when discussing making time to spend with people. Don't overestimate what that means in terms of quantity.

The vast majority of people understand the value of their boss's time, and just 15 focused, tuned-in minutes can really make a difference, particularly face-to-face.

When I bring up displaying your own fallibility to most of my leader clients, they usually groan or acknowledge that, yes, it makes sense, but avoid doing it anyway, at least initially. We are not talking about revealing your deepest, darkest secrets and insecurities here. Remember, the truth of the situation is you are fallible. Being authentic is about being truthful. You can acknowledge your own fallibility by asking questions. You can talk about mistakes you have made in the past. Find your own way of acknowledging that you don't have all the answers, and communicate this both verbally and nonverbally. Status differences influence the way people see each other. This is easy to forget, particularly if you have more status. Lower-status people often over-estimate the power of higher-status people.

Let's go back to the case of Ken and Project Turn Key. When Ken did meet with the project team live and in person, he told them directly that his boss was likely to refuse "the ask" for another $2 million. He related experiences in the past in which he had asked her for more funding without any warning like this one. Every time, she had told him absolutely not and to "go figure it out." By sharing this with his team, Ken was openly acknowledging his fallibility. When he and I debriefed his live meeting with the team, he said every single team member was openly shocked that his boss was likely to say "absolutely not" to him. The team had overestimated Ken's power. It blew their minds to think that he too had a boss who could simply say no to him. Ken told the absolute truth and acknowledged his fallibility in two sentences.

Highlighting failures as learning opportunities and holding people accountable for transgressions may seem mutually exclusive on first blush. They are not. One without the other will contribute to your lack of success. The truth is not usually one-dimensional once you get more than one person working on a project or in an organization.

An event in the life of a team can be both a failure and an opportunity for learning. The skill of framing events as both learning opportunities and failures is important for authentic leaders to develop. First, you must openly acknowledge the failure. In Ken's situation, he and the team actually walked through the negative implications of the project not being finished by the end of the calendar year. That made the failure very real. Then, Ken said, "We are not likely to get the extra $2 million or to finish by the end of the year as we promised." Toward the close of that very long and exhausting meeting, Ken asked, "What have we as a team learned from this?" They wrote down the lessons and circulated them via e-mail. One team member took the initiative and created a poster of three critical lessons for each team member to keep in their space. The whole experience brought the team much closer. I caught up with a member of that team two years later who recounted to me how that experience was deeply meaningful to her.

Finally, clarify boundaries and expectations. This is simple but not easy. Create ground rules for the team. Include specific rules, such as "admit your mistakes quickly" or "relate bad news in person." Creating the rules is easy. Keeping them top of mind and living them out is the tough part. Environments in which the rules are clear feel much safer than environments in which the rules are not articulated clearly. This is just as true for adults as it is for kids. You also need to create "accountability guardrails" for the team. What happens when someone violates the rules? How will it be addressed? What is the procedure? This accountability process, or clarifying the guardrails, is critical for making the ground rules real.

Next, we move from the practical aspects of cultivating conditions for truth telling as an authentic leader and into the broader territory of human virtue and character.

⁂

IN SEARCH OF A VIRTUE BUZZ

I want to challenge your notion of virtue, character, and good behavior for its own sake. You may have recoiled at the very mention of the word *virtue* or *character* and wondered if Karissa was going to get preachy. Our U.S. culture, at least, has been heavily influenced by puritanical notions, and most people look beleaguered and/or somber at the very mention of words like *character, virtue,* or *moral education* in the abstract. The psychological research, however, draws a stark contrast to those somber states when we examine what really happens when we see human virtue in action compared with talking about it. Let's look at how this works in real life.

It was 6:30 in the morning and my "to do list" was calling me loudly while I stood in line at the local Panera Bread, looking forward to the hazelnut coffee and the egg white, spinach, and avocado breakfast power sandwich. I was telling myself that a project was going to be totally derailed if I could not get a client to return my call today. I counted 15 people in front of me as my mind moved into the present situation and, unfortunately, into a state of mild panic and irritation. A haze of frustration and negativity pervaded the line, which was moving at an agonizingly slow pace. We all groaned as we heard the cashier instruct a new employee how to key in a latte. Now we knew what was going on here. We were going to be here for a while. Was I going to have a caffeine-deprivation headache before I got through this line? Needless to say, based on what we learned in Chapter 11, I was not in a state of authentic leadership as I was not "other focused" at all!

Then, something extraordinary happened. A woman six people ahead of me in line said to the person in front of her, "hold my place for a second." Then she left the line to help an older gentleman whose hands were shaky get his coffee to his table. A hush fell over the entire line, as we were all transfixed by her virtuous behavior. I personally felt a rush of warmth in my chest and a lump in my throat as I watched this woman demonstrate virtue somewhere around 6:40 AM in the slow coffee line. The frustration hum emanating from all 15 of us subsided for a moment, and you could feel the uplift of energy in the quiet. I felt a positive buzz as I watched this ordinary woman simply help this older gentleman get his coffee and settle at his table. I noticed the buzz and intentionally savored it for a while before my inner critic kicked in and asked, "Why didn't you think to do that?" and then just as quickly reassured me that it really wasn't that big of a deal.

But it was a big deal. Psychologists have a name for the buzz or positive state that I experienced in the coffee line. I experienced a state of *elevation* in a very ordinary human situation. The state of elevation is an emotional response that happens when we witness a virtuous act of kindness that someone else does for the benefit of another human being.

We are lifted up higher and into a more positive frame of mind psychologically.

This is what I call a *virtue buzz*. In order to enjoy it more and have an even more positive experience, slow down and savor it before your mind just moves on. For evolutionary purposes, our brains are wired so that negative emotions are intense and capture our full attention. Think about the well-known fight-or-flight stress response you experienced the last time you had a close call while driving, or thought you were going to get pulled over for speeding. However, these more subtle virtue buzzes—and positive emotions in general—are easy to miss and dismiss.

We experience this state of elevation as a result of witnessing the best of human nature or virtue in action. We are simply noticing other people doing good things. The state of elevation was described by Jonathan Haidt and Sara Algoe[7] in a series of rigorous studies with college students from the University of Virginia. Some of the actual prompts they used are listed below.

Let's give you a flavor of the experiment. Take three minutes and write a brief response to each of the prompts below. Don't rush through here. You could miss something important that will really revolutionize the way you think about being an authentic leader, or better yet, a virtue buzz.

1. Please think of a specific time when you saw someone demonstrating humanity's higher or better nature. Please pick a situation in which you were not the beneficiary, that is, you saw someone doing something good, honorable, or charitable for someone else.

2. Please think of a specific time when someone did something really good for you. Please pick a situation in which you benefited because of someone else's kindness, helpfulness, or generosity.

3. Please think of a specific time when you witnessed someone overcoming adversity. Please pick a situation in which someone else successfully overcame an obstacle or handicap.

How did each of the prompts impact you? What were the differences between your responses to the three? In my coaching practice, I use such prompts and pay attention to my clients without ever directly asking "how do you feel?" In fact, the best way to kill a virtue buzz in the work setting is to directly ask how someone feels. Maybe you can get by with it, but I am a psychologist, and the minute I ask how anyone feels, I know I can expect jokes and defenses. But I have other methods.

The researchers were attempting to understand how what they called "other praising" emotions worked. Other praising simply means positive feelings about another human being. The three other praising emotions identified were elevation, gratitude, and admiration. Of the prompts above, the first one is designed to provoke elevation—perhaps we could call it "the Panera prompt." The second prompt above was used to provoke gratitude, and the third prompt was used to provoke feelings of admiration.

The research psychologists were also too smart to ask directly how the participants were feeling, but instead constructed a sophisticated questionnaire, which measured physiological details such as a lump in the throat or a tightening of the chest. Physiological details allowed researchers to record emotional responses without the results becoming totally contaminated by rationalization and thinking. Their hypothesis, that seeing others doing virtuous things elicited positive emotions, was subjected to rigorous scientific analysis. The conclusion was clear: Seeing others behave in ways that are morally virtuous, kind, or admirable provokes the positive emotions of elevation, gratitude, and admiration.

As we all know, emotions make us want to take action. Haidt and Algoe identified specific action tendencies generated by the three different states. The emotion of elevation makes us want to do things for the good of the team or the collective. Gratitude provokes us to improve the relationship with the person who did something kind for us. And admiration provokes a desire to be a better version of ourselves. Yes, you read that right: Seeing someone else be excellent makes the individuals simply watching want to improve and be excellent, too. Such positive emotions have been clearly linked more generally to what renowned positive psychology researcher Barbara Frederickson[8] has termed a *broaden and build mind-set*. Just like it sounds, in the broaden and build mind-set, people see a wider range of options for behavior and are much more open to possibility. In other words, you don't have to be cynical or irritated while standing in a long line. This mind-set is clearly connected to a wide range of positive emotions including elevation, gratitude, and admiration.

What does all of this have to do with authentic leadership? If you as a leader demonstrate virtuous or good behavior in ordinary ways, do nice things for the members of your team, and demonstrate competence and excellence, you are likely provoking this broaden and build state in your followers.

Think about that for a minute. Demonstrating your competence or doing your job with excellence along with being a good example literally provokes people into an emotional state in which they want to get better. That motivation to get better is a precursor to high performance in any field.

But you can't fake it and do this stuff in a check-it-off-the-list manner. You have to slow down enough to notice that someone needs help getting to the table with their coffee. You have to notice that someone on your team is having a rough time. One of my clients keeps his entire organization of 5,000 people in a constant moderate gratitude buzz through his innovative and funny digital birthday cards. These cards are a genuine, authentic expression of him as the quirky, funny, and utterly unique human being that he is. He is also a master of his functional area and stays on top of every development in his fast-changing field of expertise.

The idea of being in a generally positive emotional state at work is something we would all sign up for. Emotions are more contagious than the common cold. Think about a toxic coworker who is always negative, and you'll know what I mean by contagious. You need emotional Purell^{TM} after interacting with some individuals. The good news is that positive emotions are contagious, too. Having people want to improve, look out for the team, and develop strong relationships are powerful levers for creating great places to work. An act of virtue need not be grand, heroic, or big. An act of virtue can be as simple as saying "how are you?" and really listening to the answer, or holding the door open for someone. Creating a generally positive work environment in which people have quality relationships actually sets up the conditions for people to become more authentic instead of squelching themselves and just getting through the day. The most interesting thing about the virtue buzz is that it lifts the spirits of everyone involved. The person who commits the act of kindness or virtue may actually benefit the most from it in terms of an overall emotional mood improvement. Doing good literally makes us feel better. Cheers to regular virtue buzzes!

SELF-DEFINING MOMENTS

Authentic leaders are committed to the pursuit of the truth about their businesses, themselves, and other people. A virtue like pursuing the truth is not a skill-based strength like communicating clearly or having a good mind for math. Virtue goes deeper than skill. Sometimes authentic leaders practice virtues like telling the truth for the sake of telling the truth. Such times serve as self-defining moments in the journey toward becoming more authentic.

Now for one final tale from my extraordinary clientele. I was working with a client, Len, in a stretch role. Stretch roles are usually pressure-filled, hard, and highly visible. They are essentially designed to test people. Len was not doing well in such a role. Things were going so badly that his boss, Bryan, did not see another promotion in my client's future at this company. (Don't feel too sorry for Len, as he was already at a very high level.) Bryan called me one day with a dilemma. Should he tell this high-flying, highly ambitious person, my client, the truth that he was not likely to be promoted past his current level? Bryan explained to me that he would need Len's technical skill and expertise in order to complete several transactions key to the future of the business within the next year. If Bryan told him this truth, Len had a great résumé and could very well leave. Len's departure would make the next year more difficult for the entire team, and potentially negatively impact the results.

What would you do? Bryan told my client the truth within a month. He took the risk that Len would leave. The essence of being an authentic leader as Bryan defined it meant looking out for his people was more important to him than the personal costs of figuring out how to do the work in his absence. That being said, Bryan was prudent and had a plan B ready in the event that Len left abruptly. The plan B would require much more of Bryan's time and attention and additional people he did not know well, but he was prepared for the worst.

This particular story has a happy ending. Len did not leave the company and he has a great deal of respect for his former boss who gave him the horrible news. In fact, the news prompted Len to take stock and reevaluate what he wanted out of his life and career. After the shock wore off, Len realized that actually, he didn't really want to be in a higher-level role. He wanted to invest more time and energy with his two teenage children, as he felt he had missed a lot of time with them through the years. Not hustling for his next promotion would grant him that time. In this case, the boss's authenticity impacted my client and he became more honest about what he really wanted out of his whole life, not just his work life.

Alas, this final client tale and many others are far more complicated than a simple virtue buzz. However, watching all of this transpire was inspiring for me at a deep level and obviously, for my client. That is the impact of such truth telling and authenticity, particularly when it is so carefully chosen and carries personal risk for a person of power who could so easily make another choice without anyone knowing. It requires practicing virtue when you simply need to slow down and notice what is going on around you. You should also practice virtues that are part of who you are, such as truth-telling when it is more difficult and challenging.

❦

THE WORKOUTS

- As you may remember, Martin Seligman and Christopher Peterson completed an ambitious work designed to organize human virtue and character that culminated in a list of 24 character strengths: creativity, curiosity, judgment, love of learning, perspective, bravery, perseverance, honesty, zest, love, kindness, social intelligence, teamwork, fairness, leadership, forgiveness, humility, prudence, self-regulation, appreciation of beauty and excellence, gratitude, hope, humor, and spirituality.

  Pick one and practice as you go about your daily routine for one week.

- Understanding more about the dynamics of trust is helpful for everyone. Part of that is becoming more aware of how you decide whom to trust and whom not to trust. That will help you understand how others make similar calculations. We learned that trust consists of integrity, ability, and benevolence. Think about a person you really trust. How would you rate him/her on integrity, ability, and benevolence? What evidence do you have to support your view?

- In this chapter we learned about five leadership behaviors that contribute to psychological safety. Those included being approachable and accessible, displaying your own fallibility, highlighting failures as learning opportunities, holding people accountable, and clarifying expectations. How have you as a leader practiced those behaviors within the last month? Look for ways to practice all of them as part of your daily routine. Are you better at one of them than the others? Which one do you try to avoid doing? You know what that means: You need to do that one!

Conclusion

Being an authentic leader is about determining who you are in your own way and making the contributions only you can make. The process does involve tough choices, hard work, and struggle. Remember to have fun, though, and savor those virtue buzzes along the way. In the immortal words of Dr. Seuss:[9]

> Today you are You, that is truer than true. There is no one alive who is more Youer than You.

Notes

Chapter 1

1. Peter Drucker, "Managing Oneself," *Harvard Business Review* (1999) 77(2), 64–75.
2. Edgar H. Schein, *Organizational Culture and Leadership* (San Francisco: Jossey-Bass, 2004).
3. Susan Harter, *Handbook of Positive Psychology*, ed. C.R. Snyder and Shane J. Lopez (Oxford: Oxford University Press, 2002), 382–394.
4. Bill George and Peter Sims, *True North: Discover Your Authentic Leadership* (San Francisco: Jossey-Bass, 2007).
5. Gareth Jones and Rob Goffee, *Why Should Anyone Be Led By You?* (Boston: Harvard University Press, 2006).
6. Peter Drucker, "Managing Oneself," *Harvard Business Review* (1999) 77(2), 64–75.
7. James C. Collins, *Good to Great: Why Some Companies Make the Leap . . . and Others Don't* (New York: HarperBusiness, 2001).
8. Amy C. Edmondson, *Teaming: How Organizations Learn, Innovate, and Compete in the Knowledge Economy* (San Francisco: Jossey-Bass, 2012).
9. Ron Zemke, Claire Raines, and Bob Filipczak, *Generations at Work: Managing the Clash of Veterans, Boomers, Xers, and Nexters in Your Workplace* (New York: AMACOM, 2000).
10. H. James Gilmore and Joseph B. Pine, *The Experience Economy Work Is Theatre & Every Business a Stage* (Boston: Harvard University Press, 1999).
11. Barbara L. Fredrickson, *Positivity: Top-notch Research Reveals the 3-to-1 Ratio That Will Change Your Life* (New York: Three Rivers/Crown Publisher, 2009).
12. Laura A. King, "The Health Benefits of Writing About Life Goals," *Personality and Social Psychology Bulletin* (2001 27(7)), 798–807.

Chapter 2

1. From *On Becoming a Leader* by Warren G. Bennis, copyright © 1989. Reprinted by permission of Basic Books, a member of The Perseus Books Group.
2. Frank Capra, *It's a Wonderful Life,* dir. Frank Capra. (Hollywood, California: Liberty Films, 1946), film.

3. Carol Gallagher, *Going to the Top: A Road Map for Success from America's Leading Women Executives* (New York: Viking, 2001).

4. Madeleine Albright, *Read My Pins: Stories from a Diplomat's Jewel Box* (New York: HarperCollins, 2009).

5. Walter Isaacson, *Steve Jobs* (New York: Simon & Schuster, 2011).

6. Ralph Waldo Emerson, *Essays: First Series* (Boston: James Munroe and Company, 1841).

7. Dale Buss, "9 Ways to Get the Board behind Your Disruptive Strategies," *Chief Executive* (2015) http://chiefexecutive.net/9-ways-to-get-the-board-behind-your-disruptive-strategies, accessed July 15, 2015.

8. Robert Safian, "This is Generation Flux: Meet the Pioneers of the New (and Chaotic) Frontier of Business," *Fast Company* (January, 9, 2012) http://www.fastcompany.com/1802732/generation-flux-meet-pioneers-new-and-chaotic-frontier-business, accessed July 15, 2015.

9. John H. Zenger and Joseph Folkman, *The Extraordinary Leader: Turning Good Managers into Great Leaders* (New York: McGraw-Hill, 2002).

10. Brené Brown, *The Gifts of Imperfection: Let Go of Who You Think You're Supposed to Be and Embrace Who You Are* (Center City, MN: Hazelden, 2010).

11. Sheryl Sandberg with Nell Scovell. *Lean In: Women, Work, and the Will to Lead* (New York: Knopf Doubleday Publishing Group, 2013).

12. John Goldstone, *Monty Python's The Meaning of Life*, dir. Terry Jones (London, United Kingdom: Celadine Films, 1983), film.

13. Rachel Feintzeig, "I Don't Have a Job. I Have a Higher Calling," *The Wall Street Journal*, February 24, 2015, http://www.wsj.com/articles/corporate-mission-statements-talk-of-higher-purpose-1424824784, accessed July 15, 2015.

14. Amy Wrzesniewski and Jane E. Dutton, "Crafting a Job: Revisioning Employees as Active Crafters of Their Work" *The Academy of Management Review*, 26(2) Apr., 2001, 179–201.

15. Christopher Peterson and Martin Seligman, *Character Strengths and Virtues* (Oxford: Oxford University Press, 2004).

16. David Brooks, *The Road to Character*, (Random House, 2015).

17. Marie Kondo, *The Life-changing Magic of Tidying Up: The Japanese Art of Decluttering and Organizing* (Berkeley, California: Ten Speed Press, 2014).

CHAPTER 3

1. Ralph Waldo Emerson, *Essays: First Series* (Boston: James Munroe and Company, 1841).

2. Maria Sirois, Psy.D. quote from Teaching for Transformation online course, spring 2015, www.MariaSirois.com.

3. Jim C. Collins and Jerry I. Porras, *Built to Last: Successful Habits of Visionary Companies* (New York: Harper Business, 2004).

4. Joseph Badaracco, *Defining Moments: When Managers Must Choose between Right and Right* (Boston, Massachusetts: Harvard Business School Press, 1997).

5. Bill George and Peter Sims, *True North: Discover Your Authentic Leadership.* (San Francisco, California: Jossey-Bass, 2007).

6. Galit Eilam and Boas Shamir, "'What's Your Story?' A Life-Stories Approach to Authentic Leadership Development," *The Leadership Quarterly* 16 (2005), 395–417.

7. Morgan McCall, Michael Lombardo, and Ann Morrison, *The Lessons of Experience: How Successful Executives Develop on the Job* (Lexington, KY Lexington Books, 1988).

8. Brian Grazer, *Liar Liar,* dir. Tom Shadyac (Universal City, California: Universal Pictures, 1997), film.

9. Bella DePaulo, *The Hows and Whys of Lies* (Lexington, KY CreateSpace Independent Publishing Platform, 2010).

10. Warren Bennis, *On Becoming a Leader* (Reading, PA: Addison-Wesley Publication, 1989).

11. Patrick J. Doyle, "How Pizza Became a Growth Stock," *The Wall Street Journal* (March 14, 2015) http://www.wsj.com/articles/the-weekend-interview-with-j-patrick-doyle-how-pizza-became-a-growth-stock-1426286353, accessed December 19, 2015.

CHAPTER 4

1. Niccoló Machiavelli, *The Prince* (New York: Alfred A. Knopf, 1992).

2. Jim Collins, *Good to Great: Why Some Companies Make the Leap . . . and Others Don't* (New York: HarperBusiness, 2001).

3. Jim Collins and Morten T. Hansen, *Great by Choice: Uncertainty, Chaos, and Luck Why Some Thrive Despite Them All* (New York: HarperCollins Publishers, 2011).

4. Max Weber, *The Theory of Social and Economic Organization* (New York: Free Press, 1947).

5. Robert J. House and Jane Howell, "Personality and Charismatic Leadership," *The Leadership Quarterly* (1992 3(2)), 81–108.

6. Mansour Javidan, Paul Varella, and David Waldman, "Charismatic Leadership at the Strategic Level: A New Application of Upper Echelons Theory," *The Leadership Quarterly* (2004 15(3)), 355–380.

7. Michael H. Kernis and Brian M. Goldman, "A Multicomponent Conceptualization of Authenticity: Theory and Research," *Advances in Experimental Social Psychology* (2006 38), 283–357.

8. Reprinted with permission of the publisher. From *Turning to One Another: Simple Conversations to Restore Hope to the Future,* copyright © 2009 by Margaret J. Wheatley, Berrett-Koehler Publishers, Inc., San Francisco, CA. All rights reserved. www.bkconnection.com

9. Richard Christie and Florence L. Geis, *Studies in Machiavellianism* (New York: Academic Press, 1970).
10. Bill George and Peter Sims, *True North: Discover Your Authentic Leadership* (San Francisco: Jossey-Bass, 2007).
11. Carol Dweck, *Mindset: The New Psychology of Success* (New York: Random House, 2006).
12. William C. Carter, *The Proust Questionnaire* (New York: Assouline, 2005).

CHAPTER 5

1. Michael H. Kernis and Brian M. Goldman, "A Multicomponent Conceptualization of Authenticity: Theory and Research," *Advances in Experimental Social Psychology* (2006 38), 283–357.
2. Fred Walumbwa, Bruce Avolio, William Gardner, Tara Wernsing, and Suzanne Peterson, "Authentic Leadership: Development and Validation of a Theory-Based Measure," *Journal of Management* (2008 34(1)), 89–126.
3. Robert Goffee and Gareth Jones, *Why Should Anyone Be Led by You? What It Takes to Be an Authentic Leader* (Boston: Harvard Business School Press, 2006).
4. Erving Goffman, *Presentations of Self in Everyday Life* (New York: Anchor Books, 1959).
5. Mark Snyder, "Self-monitoring of Expressive Behavior," *Journal of Personality and Social Psychology* (1974 30(4)), 526–537.
6. Brian R. Little, *Me, Myself, and Us: The Science of Personality and the Art of Well-being* (New York: PublicAffairs, 2014).
7. Daniel Nettle, *Personality: What Makes You the Way You Are* (Oxford: Oxford University Press, 2007).
8. Dan P. McAdams, *The Person: An Introduction to the Science of Personality Psychology* (Hoboken, N.J.: Wiley, 2009).
9. Leon Festinger, *A Theory of Cognitive Dissonance* (Stanford: Stanford University Press, 1962).

CHAPTER 6

1. Reprinted with the permission of Simon & Schuster, Inc. from *A Curious Mind: The Secret to a Bigger Life* by Brian Grazer and Charles Fishman. Copyright © 2015 by Brian Grazer. All rights reserved.
2. Doris Kearns Goodwin, *Team of Rivals: The Political Genius of Abraham Lincoln* (New York: Simon & Schuster, 2005).
3. Michael H. Kernis and Brian M. Goldman, "A Multicomponent Conceptualization of Authenticity: Theory and Research," *Advances in Experimental Social Psychology* (2006 38), 283–357.

4. Fred Walumbwa, Bruce Avolio, William Gardner, and Tara Wernsing, "Authentic Leadership: Development and Validation of a Theory-Based Measure," *Journal of Management* (2008 34(1)), 89–126.

5. J. Richard Hackman, *Leading Teams: Setting the Stage for Great Performances* (Boston: Harvard Business School Press, 2002).

6. Jonno Hanafin, http://www.corecontext.co.uk/who-we-are/jonno-hanafin, accessed August 2, 2015.

7. Irving L. Janis, *Victims of Groupthink; a Psychological Study of Foreign-policy Decisions and Fiascoes* (Boston: Hougton, Mifflin, 1972).

8. George A. Kelly, *A Theory of Personality; the Psychology of Personal Constructs* (New York: W.W. Norton, 1963).

9. John S. Hammond, Ralph L. Keeney, and Howard Raiffa, "The Hidden Traps in Decision Making," *Harvard Business Review* (September-October 1998), 47–58.

10. Amos Tversky and Daniel Kahneman, "The Framing of Decisions and the Psychology of Choice," *Science New Series* (1982 211(4481)), 453–458.

CHAPTER 7

1. Excerpt(s) from *American Icon: Alan Mulally and the Fight to Save Ford Motor Company* by Bryce G. Hoffman, copyright © 2012 by Bryce G. Hoffman. Used by permission of Crown Business, an imprint of the Crown Publishing Group, a division of Penguin Random House LLC. All rights reserved.

2. Tim Cook, "Tim Cook Speaks Up." *Bloomberg Business*, October 30, 2014. Used with permission of Bloomberg L.P. Copyright@ 2015. All rights reserved.

3. Jonas Rivera, *Inside Out*, dir. Pete Docter (New York: Walt Disney Pictures and Pixar Animation Studios, 2015) film.

4. Don Tapscott and David Ticoll, *The Naked Corporation: How the Age of Transparency Will Revolutionize Business* (New York: Free Press, 2003).

5. Warren Bennis and James O'Toole, "A Culture of Candor," *Harvard Business Review*, June 17, 2009, Reprint R0906F.

6. Bill George and Peter Sims, *True North: Discover Your Authentic Leadership* (San Francisco: Jossey-Bass, 2007).

7. Erving Goffman, *The Presentation of Self in Everyday Life* (Garden City, N.Y.: Doubleday, 1959).

8. Lucy Kellaway, "Microsoft Mission Statement: So Many Words, Most of Them Empty," *Financial Times* (July 6, 2015) http://www.ft.com/intl/cms/s/0/f00b0b08-1f4f-11e5-aa5a-398b2169cf79.html#axzz3umxTFDs4, accessed July 7, 2015.

CHAPTER 8

1. *New American Standard Bible, Matthew 7:3–5* (La Habra, CA: Foundation Publications, 1973).

2. Excerpt(s) from *The Righteous Mind: Why Good People Are Divided by Politics and Religion* by Jonathan Haidt, copyright © 2012 by Jonathan Haidt. Used by permission of Pantheon Books, an imprint of the Knopf Doubleday Publishing Group, a division of Penguin Random House LLC. All rights reserved.

3. Stephen Woolley, *The Crying Game,* dir. Neil Jordan (London, England: Palace Pictures, 1992) film.

4. Michael H. Kernis and Brian M. Goldman, "A Multicomponent Conceptualization of Authenticity: Theory and Research." *Advances in Experimental Social Psychology* (2006 38), 283–357.

5. Fred Walumbwa, Bruce Avolio, William Gardner, and Tara Wernsing, "Authentic Leadership: Development and Validation of a Theory-Based Measure," *Journal of Management* (2008 34(1)), 89–126.

6. Bill George and Peter Sims, *True North: Discover Your Authentic Leadership* (San Francisco: Jossey-Bass, 2007).

7. Anne Colby and Lawrence Kohlberg, *The Measurement of Moral Judgment* (Cambridge: Cambridge University Press, 1987).

8. Jonathan Haidt, *The Righteous Mind: Why Good People Are Divided by Politics and Religion* (New York: Pantheon Books, 2012).

9. Mike Judge, John Altschuler, and Dave Krinsky, *Silicon Valley* (Los Angeles, HBO, 2015) TV series.

10. Shannon, Polly and Kathryn Britton, *Character Strengths Matter: How to Live a Full Life* (Philadelphia, Positive Psychology News, 2015).

CHAPTER 9

1. Sheena Iyengar, *The Art of Choosing* (New York: Twelve, 2010).

2. Susan Cain, *Quiet: The Power of Introverts in a World That Can't Stop Talking* (New York: Broadway Books, 2012).

3. Boas Shamir and Gamit Eilam, "What's Your Story?" *The Leadership Quarterly* (16 2005), 395–417.

4. Herminia Ibarra, *Act Like a Leader, Think Like a Leader* (Boston: Harvard Business Review Press 2015).

5. Amy Cuddy, "Your Body Language Shapes Who You Are," (2012). TED Global Conference, https://www.ted.com/talks/amy_cuddy_your_body_language_shapes_who_you_are?language=en, accessed August 14, 2015.

6. Susan Harter, *Handbook of Positive Psychology*, ed. C.R. Snyder and Shane J. Lopez (Oxford: Oxford University Press, 2002), 382–394.

7. Ellen J. Langer, *Mindfulness: 25th Anniversary Edition*, 2014 Boston: Da Capo Press.

8. Andre Agassi, *Open: An Autobiography* (New York: Alfred A. Knopf, 2009).

CHAPTER 10

1. Eric Schmidt and Jonathan Rosenberg, *How Google Works* (New York: Grand Central Publishing, 2014).
2. Edgar H. Schein, *Organizational Culture and Leadership* (San Francisco: Jossey-Bass Publishers, 1985).
3. James S. Kunen, "Enron's Vision (and Values) Thing," *New York Times* (January 19, 2002), http://www.nytimes.com/2002/01/19/opinion/enron-s-vision-and-values-thing.html, accessed: September 1, 2015.

CHAPTER 11

1. Robert E. Quinn, *Building the Bridge As You Walk on It: A Guide for Leading Change* (New York: Jossey-Bass, 2014).
2. Gareth Jones and Rob Goffee, *Why Should Anyone Be Led By You?* (Boston: Harvard University Press, 2000).
3. Paramahansa Yogananda, *Autobiography of a Yogi* (New York: The Philosophical Library, 1946).
4. E. Tory Higgens, "Self-Discrepancy: A Theory Relating Self and Affect," *Psychological Review* (1987 94(3)), 319–340.
5. Richard E. Boyatzis and Kleio Akrivou, "The Ideal Self as the Driver of Intentional Change," *The Journal of Management Development* (2006 25(7)), 634–642.
6. Brittney Helmrich, "30 Ways to Define Leadership." *Business News Daily* (June 19, 2015). http://www.businessnewsdaily.com/3647-leadership-definition.html, accessed September 1,2015.

CHAPTER 12

1. Martin Seligman's Twitter handle self-description, 2015 https://twitter.com/martinseligman, accessed September 10, 2015.
2. Dr. Robert W. Terry, Founder, The AWL Group. *Authentic Leadership: Courage in Action* (Jossey-Bass, San Francisco, 1993).
3. Daniel Roth, "Jack Welch Says Only Two Words Matter for Leaders Today: Truth and Trust." LinkedIn (April 21, 2015), https://www.linkedin.com/pulse/truth-trust-crap-how-jack-welch-looks-leadership-today-daniel-roth, accessed September 15, 2015
4. Penelope Greenberg, Ralph H. Greenberg, and Yvonne Antonucci, "Creating and Sustaining Trust in Virtual Teams," *Business Horizons* (2007 50), 325–33.
5. Amy C. Edmondson, *Teaming: How Organizations Learn, Innovate, and Compete in the Knowledge Economy* (San Francisco: Jossey-Bass, 2012), 139.
6. Jane E. Dutton, *Energize Your Workplace: How to Create and Sustain High-Quality Connections at Work* (San Francisco: Jossey-Bass, 2003).

7. Jonathan Haidt and Sara B. Algoe, "Witnessing Excellence in Action: The 'Other Praising' Emotions of Elevation, Gratitude, and Admiration," *Journal of Positive Psychology* (2009 4(2)), 105–127. Reprinted by permission of the publisher Taylor & Francis Ltd, http://www.tandfonline.com.

8. Barbara L. Fredrickson, *Positivity: Top-Notch Research Reveals the 3-to-1 Ratio That Will Change Your Life* (New York: Three Rivers/Crown Publisher, 2009).

9. Dr. Seuss (Theodor Seuss Geisel), *Happy Birthday to You* (New York: Random House, 1959).

ACKNOWLEDGMENTS

I always read the acknowledgments section thinking that I will understand something about the person I am about to get to know by reading their book. I always marvel at how many people are being thanked for a job that I imagined as that person sitting alone in a room with a typewriter like Hemingway. But I was very wrong in my visual imagination. The sitting-alone part is only part of the process. Writing a book is a grand, audacious thing, as opposed to just another task, and it takes multiple teams. I find myself not knowing where to start. Therefore, I will just start.

I want to thank my wife and life partner, Ginger Ward, for her unwavering belief in me over the last 27 years. It has been quite a journey and you are both my rock who calms me down and my spark plug who ignites me toward more action when my natural tendency would be to sit and think too long. My father, Ernest Thacker, who saw potential in me at every turn even when it wasn't there. Kay Keenan, who has brought her considerable and varied gifts to the table willingly and jumped in to help at every phase of this process in any way that she could. A team member like Kay is invaluable. Thank you to Elena Rocanelli Veale for her diligence in tracking down a million references and helping me see the work through the eyes of a college student. Thanks to Ken Lizotte and Elena Petricone of Emerson Consulting Group. Ken, your calm demeanor and admonition to keep plugging away made it possible for me to get through the proposal phase and the writing days. Elena, you have a strong voice of your own and a gift for hearing ideas and amplifying the voices of others. Thanks to Carroll Ivy Laurence for taking on the formidable task of educating me about the power of social media. I would like to thank Drew Fennell for her friendship and more specifically for the enthusiastic reading of the early drafts and approaching it with glee as if it were an unfolding drama like a Shonda Rhimes TV show. Thanks to my friend Lisa Goodman, the attorney and equestrian, who branched out and provided the key psychological counsel involved in writing: "You just do it," and she said it with such authority that I just believed her. I am grateful that Phoebe Atkinson came into my life as a friend and colleague through the Certificate in Positive Psychology program at just the right time. Phoebe, I have never met anyone who was more skillful at encouraging others to find the courage to be a better version of themselves. A special shout-out to the founders of the Certificate in Positive Psychology (CIPP) program: Megan McDonough, Tal Ben-Shahar, and Maria Sirois. The CIPP program really has changed and enlivened this hard-core cynic and you three and your model of teaming inspire us all. Megan, with your mindful bias toward action and theories of adaptive execution, you embody the authentic leadership that is so relevant to today's business challenges. Tal, your passion for psychology and the science of human behavior helped me reconnect to my heartfelt passion for learning that had gone dormant. Maria, your authenticity, fierce vulnerability, and gift for storytelling inspired me to get real and lighten my psychological load as I was staring the big 50 in the face.

Last but certainly not least, thanks to Jeannene Ray and the team at Wiley for taking the risk on an unknown and believing in these ideas. Nothing is as powerful as an idea whose time has come. This notion of authenticity is an idea whose time has come again, as it is not new but particularly relevant now.

ABOUT THE AUTHOR

Dr. Karissa Thacker is a widely respected management psychologist who has served as a consultant for more than 200 Fortune 500 companies, including UPS, Best Buy, and AT&T. Her specialty is executive coaching with a focus on increased performance at work in combination with increased individual satisfaction. Her coaching method assumes that increases in effectiveness or productivity without increasing personal satisfaction are not built to last.

Karissa's background and training is in the field of psychology. She received a doctorate in psychology in 1996 from Spalding University and is a licensed psychologist. She later served as a marketing researcher at General Mills in the area of strategic growth initiatives. Her research focused on understanding consumers in international markets and advertising development. She also served as a senior consultant at RHR International, a global management consultancy specializing in executive development.

Karissa is the founder and president of Strategic Performance Solutions, Inc, a management-consulting firm focused on creating innovative solutions in the space of human performance and satisfaction at work. She also serves as adjunct faculty at the Lerner School of Business at the University of Delaware, specializing in executive development and organization effectiveness in the graduate MBA program.

She is regularly quoted in *The New York Times, The Wall Street Journal, Human Resource Executive* Online, MSNBC, and other high-profile outlets. She has become a go-to authority on authentic leadership for many top-level reporters covering these issues.

INDEX

truthfulness (*continued*)
    integrity and, 40–44
    making choices about, 33–34
    overview, 33–34
    practicing authenticity and,
        44–46
    value of honest conversation
        for relational transparency,
        104–105 (*See also* relational
        transparency)
    See also relational transparency;
        truth, pursuit of
"Turning to One Another"
    (Wheatley), 59–60
Twain, Mark, 90

U
University of Michigan, 176, 190
University of Virginia, 194
UPS, 159–160, 161–164

V
values
    espoused values, 160
    organizational culture and,
        154–155
    See also relational transparency
Varella, Paul, 56
VIA Institute on Character, 30

"virtue buzz," 192–197
virtues, "eulogy" *versus* "résumé,"
    30–31
vision, 56–57, 58

W
Waldman, David, 56
Wall Street Journal, 29
"*Wall Street Journal* test,"
    129–130
Walumba, Fred, 71, 88
weakness, as strength, 25–28
Weber, Max, 54
Welch, Jack, 53, 185
Wernsing, Tara, 71
Wheatley, Margaret, 59–60
*Why Should Anyone Be Led By
    You?* (Jones, Goffee), 7, 170

Y
"Your Body Language Shapes
    Who You Are" (Cuddy),
    143

Z
Zappos, 156
Zenger, John H., 26–27
Zimbardo, Phillip, 122–125
Zuckerberg, Mark, 28